SWU-800- 012

UNIFORMS OF RUSSIAN ARMY DURING THE YEARS 1825-1855 VOL. 12

UNDER THE REIGN OF NICHOLAS I
EMPEROR OF RUSSIA BETWEEN 1825 TO 1855
DON COSSACKS AND BLACK SEA COSSACKS

From the Viskovatov's greatest work:
"Historical description of the clothing and
arms of the Russian Army"

English translation by Mark Conrad

SOLDIERSHOP PUBLISHING

AUTHOR

Aleksandr Vasilevich Viskovatov born 22 April (4 May New Style) 1804, died 27 February (11 March) 1858 in St. Petersburg, Russian military historian. He graduated from the 1st Cadet Corps and served in the artillery, the hydrographic depot of the Naval Ministry, and then in the Department of Military Educational Institutions. He mainly studied historical artifacts and the histories of military units. Viskovatov's greatest work was the Historical Description of the Clothing and Arms of the Russian Army.

Title: **UNIFORMS OF RUSSIAN ARMY DURING THE YEARS 1825-1855. VOL. 12** -Under the reign of Nicholas I emperor of Russia between 1825-1855

By A.V.Viskovatov. Serie edit by Luca S. Cristini. First edition by Soldiershop. July 2019
Cover & Art Design: Luca S. Cristini. Plates re-colorations by Anna Cristini. ISBN code: 978-88-93274296
Published by Luca Cristini Editore, via Orio 35/4- 24050 Zanica (BG) ITALY. www.soldiershop.com

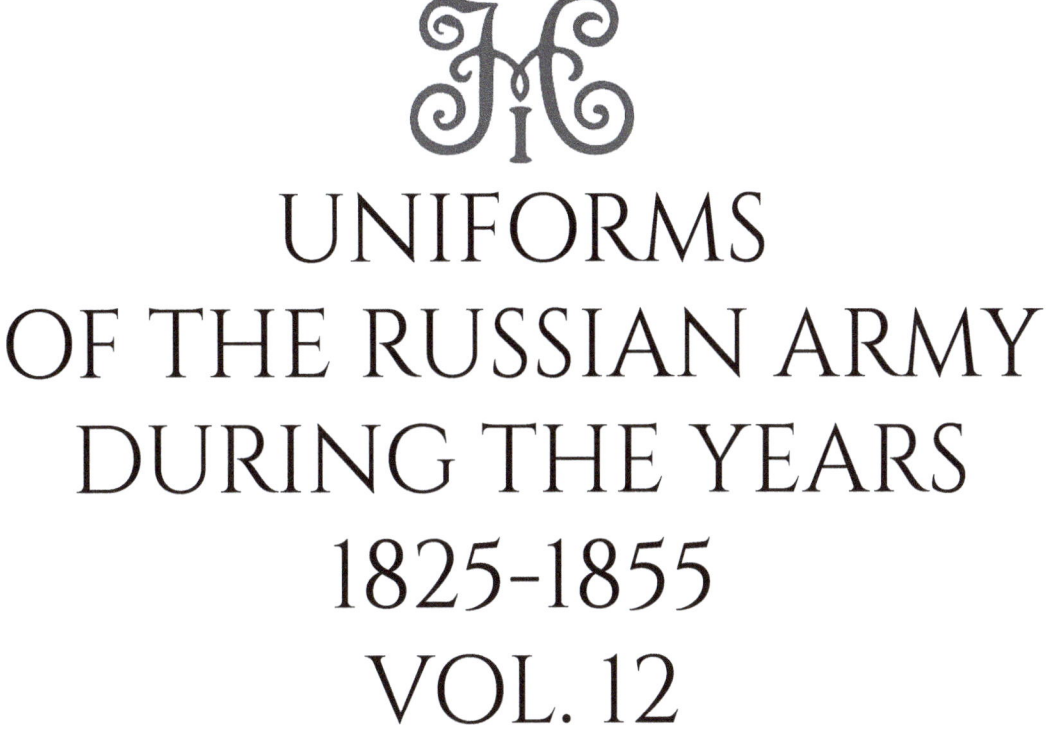

UNIFORMS
OF THE RUSSIAN ARMY
DURING THE YEARS
1825-1855
VOL. 12

UNDER THE REIGN OF NICHOLAS I EMPEROUR OF
RUSSIA BETWEEN 1825 AND 1855

*

DON COSSACKS AND BLACK SEA COSSACKS

Russian cossacks 1825-1854

HISTORICAL DESCRIPTION OF THE CLOTHING AND ARMS OF THE RUSSIAN ARMY - A.V. VISKOVATOV
(First English translation by Mark Conrad)

Soldiershop is glad to presents the complete collection of the great job made by A.V. Viskovatov dedicated to the uniforms and weapons belonging from the first Zar and Russian emperors to the Russian army during the Napoleonic period, until 1860 about. The time we considered in this volume corresponds to the reigns of Nicholas I that was the Emperor of Russia from 1825 until 1855. He was also the King of Poland and Grand Duke of Finland. He is best known as a political conservative whose reign was marked by geographical expansion, repression of dissent, economic stagnation, poor administrative policies, a corrupt bureaucracy, and frequent wars that culminated in Russia's defeat in the Crimean War of 1853–56.

Our reprint in based on the original 19th century volumes. This part is distributed at now on six volumes.

Our new edition, the first ever published in English, both on paper and digital format, boasts a large number of color plates, many of them unpublished and re-coloured by our team of expert artists and scholars of uniformology. Each volume is based on 100 color plates or more, always accompanied by the original translated text which describes the subjets of the plates.

A unique work in its genre, a must have in any respecting collection!

Aleksandr Vasilevich Viskovatov born 22 April (4 May New Style) 1804, died 27 February (11 March) 1858 in St. Petersburg, Russian military historian. He graduated from the 1st Cadet Corps and served in the artillery, the hydrographic depot of the Naval Ministry, and then in the Department of Military Educational Institutions.

He mainly studied historical artifacts and the histories of military units. Viskovatov's greatest work was the Historical Description of the Clothing and Arms of the Russian Army (Vols. 1-30, St. Petersburg, 1841-62; 2nd ed. Vols. 1-34, St. Petersburg - Novosibirsk - Leningrad, 1899-1948). This work is based on a great quantity of archival documents and contains four thousand colored illustrations.

Viskovatov was the author of Chronicles of the Russian Army (Books 1-20, St. Petersburg, 1834-42) and Chronicles of the Russian Imperial Army (Parts 1-7, St. Petersburg, 1852). He collected valuable material on the history of the Russian navy which went into A Short Overview of Russian Naval Campaigns and General Voyages to the End of the XVII Century (St. Petersburg, 1864; 2nd edition Moscow, 1946). Together with A.I. Mikhailovskii-Danilevskii he helped prepare and create the Military Gallery in the Winter Palace.

He wrote the historical military inscriptions for the walls of the Hall of St. George in the Great Palace of the Kremlin. (From the article in the Soviet Military Encyclopedia.)

CONTENTS

HISTORICAL DESCRIPTION OF THE CLOTHING AND ARMS OF THE RUSSIAN ARMY

Don Cossacks and Black Sea Cossacks 1825-1855

CHANGES IN THE UNIFORMS AND EQUIPMENT OF TEMPORARY FORCES FROM 1801 TO 1825.

CHAPTER LXXIX. I. THE DON COSSACK HOST [*DONSKOE KAZACHE VOISKO*].

a.) *The host proper, i.e. excluding the Ataman and Life-Guards Cossack Regiments and Artillery.*

1 January 1827 - In order to differentiate between ranks, officers' **epaulettes** [*epolety*] are to have small forged and stamped stars [*zvezdochki*] as established at this time for regular forces [1].

10 July 1827 - Headdresses [*shapki*] in the Don Host are to have round **pompons** [*pompony*]: for lower ranks — of white wool, for officers — silver (Illus. 1070 and 1071) [2].

7 August 1829 - **Epaulettes** on officers' uniforms are to have scaled fields [*cheshuichatoe pole*] like the pattern of epaulettes in the regular light cavalry (Illus. 1072) [3].

April 1831 - Officers without permanent positions [*za-uryad-ofitsery*] are to have small forged and stamped stars on their epaulettes like those established on 1 January 1827 in the regular light cavalry to distinguish rank [4].

26 May 1835 - By a decree [*Polozhenie*] confirmed by HIGHEST AUTHORITY regulating the Don Host, lower ranks of this host are prescribed the same uniform, weapons, and horse furniture as they had prior to this decree, except that the *chekmen* coat is discontinued. Thus: **headdress** [*shapka*] of black astrakhan [*chernaya smushka*] with a scarlet cloth bag [*vykid alago sukna*]; white headdress cords [*etishkety*] and pompons; black **neckcloth** [*galstukh*]; **jacket** [*kurtka*] of dark-blue cloth, with red cloth piping on the collar and cuffs; *sharavary* **pants** of dark-blue cloth with red lining; black nankeen **girdle** [*kushak chernoi kitaiki*]; **greatcoat** [*shinel*] of grey cloth, with a dark-blue collar; **boots** with iron spurs; **shoulder straps** [*pogony*] with a cut-out of the regimental number (from 1 to 54 inclusive); **cartridge-pouch** [*lyadunka*] of black leather, with a white metal plate [*gerb*]; a **crossbelt** [*perevyaz*] for the cartridge-pouch of black, lacquered leather, with a white metal monogram [*venzel*] and a whitened brass chain [*mednaya, otbelennaya tsepochka*]; black leather **swordbelt** [*portupeya*]; standard cossack **saddle** with saddle-blanket [*potnik*] and cover [*kryshka*]; black leather pad [*podushka*] for the saddle; saddle-cloth [*valtrap*] of dark-blue cloth; black leather valise [*chemodan*]; steel **saber** [*sablya*]; a **pistol** [*pistolet*] on a black wool cord [*shnur*] in a leather ammunition carrier [*patrontash*]; **lance-head** [*drotik*] fixed on a black shaft [*drevko*]; **bridle, harness,** and **chest-band** [*uzda, pafy i nagrudnik*] without any fittings.

Non-commissioned officers [*uryadniki*], clerks [*pisarya*], and apprentice medical orderlies [*lekarskie ucheniki*], as distinct from simple cossacks, have silver galloon on the collars and cuffs of their coats. Deputies to these non-commissioned officers [*uryadnichie pomoshniki*] wear the same galloon but only on the cuffs.

Generals and field and company-grade officers have lace bars [*petlitsy*] on the collar and cuffs. These are silver as are other distinctions for generals and officers.

For everyday use all ranks have **forage caps** [*furazhki*] of dark-blue cloth trimmed and piped [*c vykladkoyu i vypushkoyu*] as on the collar, and while in the field they have black oilskin **covers** [*chekhly iz chernoi kleenki*] for the regulation shapka headdress [5].

The following directives are established regarding the weapons for combatant lower ranks:

All non-commissioned officers and cossacks have **sabers** with iron fittings and carried on a black leather belt [*poyas*]. In view of the recognized convenience and in accordance with long-standing custom, *shashka* swords may be used instead of sabers.

Each Don regiment is to have two hundred cossacks armed with **muskets** [*ruzhya*] which, because of the character of cossack duties, are carried over the shoulder.

Regiments of the Don Host on field service are to have the same 7-line [*semilineinyi* = 0.7-inch] caliber musket as the pattern confirmed for the Black Sea Host.

In all Don regiments **lance-heads** are to be identical, with **shafts** [*s ratovyami (drevkami)*] of the prescribed dimensions finished with black paint, according to the pattern confirmed by HIGHEST AUTHORITY [6].

28 October 1836 - In all those situations for which in the regular forces the frock coat [*syurtuk*] is permitted to be worn, all generals and field and company-grade officers of the Host are to wear a **chekmen coat** without embroidery [*bez shitya*], dark blue with red piping on the collar and cuffs, and distinct from the standard host chekmen with lace bars (Illus. 1073) [7].

15 January 1837 - Girdles [*kushaki*] are not to be worn with the unembroidered chekmen established for ordinary wear on 28 October 1836 (Illus. 1073) [8].

15 July 1837 - Officers are given a new pattern **sash** [*sharf*] with a narrow, silver lace [*tesma*] body with three stripes of light-orange and black silk, as established at this time for regular forces [9].

17 December 1837 - An additional, fourth, thin twist of braid is added to officers' **epaulettes**, as in the regular forces [10].

29 April 1838 - Regiments of the Don Host are to have:

1) *For lower ranks* — **shapka headdresses** of the previous pattern but without cords; **ammunition carriers** [*patrontashi*] in place of the cartridge pouch, for 40 rounds, of black Russia leather [*yuftovaya kozha*] with a similar cover and a crossbelt made from a black, rawhide strap; **pistols** of the pattern used in the light cavalry; **pistol holders or carriers** [*chushki ili kobury*] in place of holsters [*olstredi*], of black, polished leather; pistol cords [*pistoletnye shnury*] in the same color as the edging on the uniform; the upper part of the **pistol case** [*pistoletnyi chekhol*] to the lock is of cloth the same color as the collar, while the lower part is of black polished leather; **swordbelts** are of the same kind of leather; **shashkas** (instead of sabers) have brass hilts, fittings, rings, and endpieces, in wooden scabbards wrapped with black leather; **muskets**, for mounted order, of the pattern used by the Life-Guards Black Sea Squadron, with covers, and worn on the back over the right shoulder on a black polished shoulder-strap 1 1/8 inches wide with a brass buckle; **saddle-cloths** [*valtrapy*] and **saddle-seats** [*podushki na sedla*] of the same color as the uniform, lined with linen canvas [*s kholstinnoyu podkladkoyu*] and edged (the former along the edges and the latter all around on the seam) with tape [*tesma*] 1 1/2 inches wide, made from government cloth [*kantselyarnoe sukno*], and with similar tape 16 5/8 inches long on the rear corners of the saddle-cloth; **valises** of grey cloth, 50 3/4 inches long and 22 1/4 inches in circumference, with a linen lining and four white metal **buttons** with the raised image of the regimental number (Illus. 1074, 1075, 1076, 1077, and 1078).

2.) *For officers* — **shapka headdresses** of the previous pattern but without cords; **ammunition carriers** (in place of cartridge pouches) for 20 rounds, of black morocco [*chernyi safyan*] , with a similar cover and a belt of silver lace [*tesma*] without any interwoven colors [*bez protsveta*], lined with black morocco; **pistols** of the pattern used by officers of light cavalry; **pistol holders** [*chushki*] of black morocco; silver pistol cords; the upper part of the pistol case up to the lock is of cloth the same color as the collar, while the lower part is black morocco; **swordbelts** of silver lace without any interwoven color, lined with black morocco; **shashkas** (instead of sabers) with gilt handles, mountings, rings, and endpieces, in wooden scabbards wrapped with black morocco; **saddle-cloths** and **seats** the same color as the uniform, lined with black calf-skin and edged (the former along the edge and the latter around on the seams) with lace the same color as the edging on the uniform, 1 1/4 inches wide and 9 5/8 inches long on the front corners but 15 3/4 inches long on the back ones; **valises** of grey cloth, 21 inches long and 15 3/4 inches around, with leather lining and four silver **buttons** with a raised representation of the regimental number (Illus. 1079, 1080, 1081, and 1082).

Like the lower ranks, officers are to carry **pistols** in a holder [*chushka*] attached to the back of the swordbelt on the left side. However, like the holder, cord, and case [*chekhol*], these are to be worn only in full dress [*polnaya forma*]. **Horse furniture** [*vyuki*] for lower ranks is as follows: valise and horse-cloth [*popona*] behind the saddle, the latter positioned under the valise and, together with it, fastened to the saddle with three black straps with two-sided brass buckles [*dvukhstoronyya pryazhki*] of the previous pattern, while the **greatcoat** in front of the saddle is fastened to it by three identical straps with buckles. Along with this, the manner of rolling the greatcoat and stowing additional items, as well as all uniform items, equipment, and weaponry not mentioned here, including the shapka cover, are kept without change (Illus. 1079, 1080, 1081, 1083, and 1084) [11].

6 May 1838 - When on **internal duty** with the host [*na vnutrennei po voisku sluzhbe*], cossacks of the Don Host are prescribed:

1.) For **dismounted** cossacks [*Peshim kazakam*] — forage cap of dark-blue cloth, with a red capband and piping; greatcoat of grey cloth, with a dark-blue collar; sharavary pants of grey cloth, with dark-blue piping; and a 70-inch long lance [*pika*] (Illus. 1084).

2.) For **mounted** cossacks [*Konnym kazakam*] — forage cap, greatcoat, and sharavary as when dismounted; ammunition carrier [*patrontash*], swordbelt, shashka, and saddle as for active-duty cossacks, but the last without the cloth shabraque [*cheprak*]; and a pistol (Illus. 1084) [12].

26 December 1838 - The **Instructional Cossack Regiment** [*Uchebnyi Kazachii polk*] of the the Don Host, established on this date, is prescribed the same uniform and weaponry as the other regiments of the host, with the cossacks of the regiment being armed with a shashka, musket, pistol, and lance [13].

6 October 1841 - Lower ranks of the youths [*maloletki*] assigned to serve in the **Novocherkask Hospital** [*Novocherkaskii gospital*] of the Don Host are prescribed the following uniform: *jacket* [*kurtka*] of dark-blue cloth, with red cloth piping on the collar; dark-blue cloth *sharavary* with red cloth stripes; *forage cap* of dark-blue cloth with two red cloth edges; grey cloth *greatcoat* with dark-blue cloth shoulder-straps and collar, with brass buttons; black cloth *neckcloth with a false shirtfront* [*galstukh s manishkoyu*]; polished *boots*. For summer a *jacket and sharavary* of Flemish linen [*flamskoe polotno*] are prescribed, the first with eight covered buttons down the front (Illus. 1085) [14].

2 January 1844 - There is to be a metallic **cockade** on the front of the capband of officers' forage caps, as established at this same time for officers' forage caps in the regular forces (Illus. 1086) [15].

20 May 1844 - With the general assignment of colors for **forage caps** in the War Department [*Voennoe vedomstvo*, meaning the army in general — M.C.], incorporating a few changes from the existing scheme, the forage caps in the Don Host are to be dark blue with a red capband and red piping around the top (Illus. 1086) [16].

10 January 1845 - According to the administrative regulations [*Polozhenie*] confirmed by HIGHEST AUTHORITY on this date for the **Labor Regiment** [*Rabochii polk*] of the Don Host, its personnel are to have the following uniform and armament: *field and company-grade officers* — uniform as currently used in the host, with a gilt Cyrillic letter R on the epaulettes; *non-commissioned officers* [*uryadniki*] *and corporals* [*prikaznye*] (which latter are deputies to non-commissioned officers [*uryadnichie pomoshchniki*]) — shapka headdress, chekmen, sharavary pants, forage cap, greatcoat, and shashka sword, and *cossacks* — chekmen, sharavary, girdle, forage cap, and greatcoat — as for these same ranks in the host but with the Cyrillic letter *R* on the shoulder-straps instead of a number [17].

14 April 1845 -The present jackets [*kurtki*] in the Don Host are replaced with **chekmens** of the pattern used by generals of this host when in host uniform. Along with this, while on service in the Caucasus, Don Cossack regiments are authorized to wear **shapka headdresses** of the pattern used by the Caucasian Line Cossack Host (Illus. 1087). Also, generals and field and company-grade officers are directed to wear **pistols** with lanyards [*shnurki*] only when in formation [18].

27 April 1845 - In connection with this year's 14 April uniform changes for the Don Host, the following are to be used: **chekmen** as before, dark blue in color, but of a length that is 7 inches above the knee, with red edging on the collar and cuffs, with officers also having their prescribed silver lace bars; **shapka** of black astrakhan, 7 inches high without a sunken top [*bez razvala*], with a scarlet cloth bag [*shlyk alago sukna*] lined underneath with an oilskin base; dark-blue **girdle**; **pistol case** [*chekhol*] of the previous pattern but sewn into the holder [*chushka*] that is fitted to the swordbelt on the left side (Illus. 1088, 1089, and 1090). All other components of uniform and armament, as well as horse furniture, remain unchanged [19].

29 January 1849 - For all cossack hosts the knot of the **lance sling** [*kistochka u temlyakov na pikakh*] is to be replaced with a wooden toggle [*klyapushek*], so that when firing the musket the lance is held behind the back by the sling with its toggle being thrust through the girdle (Illus. 1091) [20].

14 September 1849 - Approval is given to the pattern for officers' **percussion pistols** (Illus. 1092) [21].

7 November 1849 - Pompons [*Pompony*] are to be 9 7/8 inches in circumference [22].

Notes to the Illustrations By Mark Conrad

1070. As described in the text; the previously red pompon is now white; collar, shoulder straps, and cuffs are dark blue piped red; the saddle-cloth is dark blue with a red stripe on the edges, as well as around the seat; white sword slings; on the back of the saddle, a shiny black case underneath a grey roll held with black straps.

1071. As 1070. Black cartridge-pouch belt for the officer.

1072. Silver cords and pompon on the headdress; black girdle.

1073. Officers invariably wear white gloves. The dark-blue forage cap has a red band and piping.

1074. Here the red regimental number is visible on the shoulder strap. Black chinstrap. There appears to be a thin red stripe on the very edge of the saddle-cloth. At the rear of the saddle there is a white bag in front of a grey one, the latter over a folded, grey item; in front of the saddle is a grey roll with black straps.

1075. All black.

1076. Lace at the mouth of the case. The tassels appear to be made of light, medium, and dark strands (possibly white, blue, and red to match the uniform, or white, black, and orange which are the Czarist colors). Above the tassels the knots are striped in three colors.

1077. Black grip.

1078. All-black case.

1079. Dark swordknot, black slings.

1081. Tassels appear to be one color.

1082. Dark swordknot with a medium tassel.

1083. The officer's greatcoat has a dark-blue collar piped red. The cossack's greatcoat has dark-blue shoulder straps and collar without piping.

1084. Forage caps dark blue with a red band and piping. The saddle is dark leather. No shoulder straps on the greatcoats.

1085. All forage caps are dark blue (including the capband) with red piping at the top of the capband and at the top of the crown. The greatcoat has dark-blue shoulder straps and collar with no piping. The all-white summer uniform has white buttons.

1086. The forage cap has a red capband and piping on the crown.

1087. Dark-blue or black girdle; dark-blue shoulder straps and collar (no piping).

1088. Black sword slings for the cossack. Here the red number 12 can be seen on the shoulder strap.

1089. Tricolored tassels and knots again.

1090. Tassels not tricolored.

1091. All black except for the wooden toggle.

b.) *The Ataman HIS IMPERIAL HIGHNESS THE HEIR AND TSESAREVICH'S Regiment [Atamanskii EGO IMPERATORSKAGO VYSOCHESTVA NASLEDNIKA TSESAREVICHA polk].*[*]

(*Note: Until 29 August 1831 this regiment was titled the Cossack Ataman *HIS IMPERIAL HIGHNESS THE HEIR'S* [*Kazachii Atamanskii EGO IMPERATORSKAGO VYSOCHESTVA NASLEDNIKA*]

1 January 1827 - In order to distinguish ranks, officers' **epaulettes** are to have small, forged and stamped stars as established at this time for regular troops [23].

10 July 1827 - The shapka headdresses in the regiment are to have round **pompons**: for lower ranks — white wool, for officers — silver (Illus. 1093 and 1094) [24].

30 December 1828 - For lower ranks the dark-blue **jackets** [*kurtki*] with sky-blue piping are replaced with ones entirely sky-blue [*gol-*

uboi]. The sky-blue stripes [*lampasy*] on the **sharavary pants** are discontinued, while the lace bars [*petlitsy*] on the collar and cuffs of both the jacket and the chekmen, as well as the epaulettes, are to be white instead of sky-blue, the last items being fringed [*s bakhramoyu*] (Illus. 1095) [25].

June 1829 - Officer's uniforms — dark-blue **chekmen coats** with sky-blue piping in winter and sky-blue **jackets** in summer — are to have lace bars of the pattern used by the Life-Guards Cossack Regiment. Belts and swordbelt remain as before (Illus. 1096) [26].

7 August 1829 - **Epaulettes** are to be scaled, for lower ranks as well as for officers, the former having fringes as before, all according to the pattern for regular light cavalry [27].

6 December 1831 - Officers and lower ranks are awarded **badges for distinction** on the headdress (of white tin for lower ranks and silver for officers), with the cut-out inscription "*Za Varshavu 25 i 26 Avgusta 1831 goda*" ["For Warsaw 25 and 26 August of the year 1831"] (Illus. 1097) [28].

16 December 1831 - Lower ranks of the regiment are to have: **crossbelts**, white instead of black; **cartridge-pouches** [*lyadunki*] with a round, brass plate; **swordbelts** of Russian leather; **sabers** [*sabli*] with a brass hilt; **pistols** on a white bandolier [*pantaler*] with a hook, as in the Life-Guards Cossack Regiment; **lances** [*piki*] with sky-blue shafts (Illus. 1098). Officers are given **cartridge-pouches** of a new pattern and **cartridge-pouch belts** [*lyadunochnyya perevyazi*] made from sky-blue lace with three silver stripes and having silver fittings (Illus. 1099) [29].

10 April 1832 - The regiment is ordered to have **saddle-cloths** [*valtrapy*] as in the Life-Guards Cossack Regiment but sky-blue instead of red, and with white (silver for officers) trim (Illus. 1098 and 1099) [30].

26 May 1833 - By the Administrative Regulation [*Polozhenie*] confirmed by HIGHEST AUTHORITY governing the Don Host, the uniform, armament, and horse equipment of the lower ranks of the Ataman HIS IMPERIAL HIGHNESS THE HEIR AND TSESAREVICH'S Regiment are prescribed to be the same as prior to the Directive, namely:

Shapka headdress of black astrakhan, with a bag of light-blue [*svetlosinnii*] cloth; white cords and pompons; black **neckcloth**; dark-blue cloth **chekmen** with light-blue piping on the collar and cuffs; light-blue **jacket**; white lace bars on the chekmen and jacket; dark-blue cloth **sharavary**; white linen **girdle**; grey cloth **greatcoat** with light-blue patches on the collar and similar shoulder straps; **boots** with iron spurs; scaled iron **epaulettes** with a white fringe; **cartridge-pouch** of black lacquered leather, with a brass plate; white deerskin **crossbelt** for the cartridge-pouch; red leather **swordbelt**; standard cossack **saddle** with sweatcloth and flap; seat for the saddle of light-blue cloth, trimmed with white lace; saddlecloth of light-blue cloth, trimmed with white lace; valise of dark grey-blue cloth; horsecloth (*popona*) of grey cloth; **crossbelt** with brass and iron fittings; iron **saber** with a brass hilt and leather swordknot; standard cavalry **pistol**; lance [*drotik*] with a light-blue shaft; **bridle, harness,** and **chest straps** with brass mountings.

Non-commissioned officers [*unter-ofitsery*], clerks [*pisarya*], and apprentice medical orderlies [*lekarskie ucheniki*] have silver lace on the collars and cuffs of their uniforms, as distinct from private cossacks.

Generals and field and company-grade officers wear lace bars on their collars and cuffs, as well as other trim for generals and officers, in silver. For everyday use, all ranks have **forage caps** of light-blue cloth, with trim and piping as on the collar, while in the field they have black oilskin covers for the dress headdresses [*stroevyya shapki*] [31].

28 October 1836 - The everyday [*vsednevnyi*] **chekmen** without embroidery, introduced on this date in the Don Host and described above, is also established for officers of the Ataman HIS IMPERIAL HIGHNESS THE HEIR AND TSESAREVICH'S Regiment, but with light-blue piping on the collar and cuffs instead of red (Illus. 1100) [32].

15 January 1837 - **Girdles** [*kushaki*] are not to be worn with the everyday chekmen without embroidery established on 28 October 1836 (Illus. 1100) [33].

15 July 1837 - Officers are given a new pattern **sash** of narrow silver lace with three light-orange and black silk stripes, as established at this same time in the regular forces [34].

17 December 1837 - A fourth, narrow twist of cord is added to officers' **epaulettes** [35].

29 April 1838 - The regiment is directed to have:

1.) *For lower ranks* — **Shapka headdresses** without cords, with the standard army plate of white tin with a brass letter F in front on the shield, and with the badge for distinction awarded on 6 December 1831 above the plate, as before; iron **epaulettes** without fringes, backed with light-blue cloth; **ammunition pouches** [*patrontashi*] (instead of cartridge-pouches [*lyadunki*]) for 40 rounds, of black Russian leather, a similar lid, and a deerskin **crossbelt**; **pistols** of the pattern used in the light cavalry; **pistol holders or carriers** [*chushki ili kobury*] (instead of holsters [*olstredi*]) of shiny black leather; **pistol lanyards** of light-blue wool; the upper part of the **pistol cases** [*chekhly*] up to the lock is of light-blue cloth, while the lower part is shiny black leather; red Russian leather **swordbelts**; **shashkas** (instead of sabers) with brass handle, mountings, rings, and endpieces, in a wooden scabbard wrapped in black leather (Illus. 1101, 1102, and 1103).

2.) *For officers* — **Shapkas** without cords, with the same appointments as for lower ranks but in silver; **ammunition pouches** (instead of cartridge-pouches) of black morocco, with a cover of light-blue cloth and a **crossbelt** of light-blue silk lace, the lace having three silver stripes down the center and being backed with light-blue morocco; **pistols** of the pattern used by officers of light cavalry; **pistol holders** of black morocco; silver **pistol lanyards**; the upper part of the **pistol case** of light-blue cloth, and the lower of black morocco; **swordbelts** of light-blue silk lace with three silver stripes down the center, backed with light-blue morocco; **shashkas** (instead of sabers) with gilt handle, mountings, rings, and endpieces, in wooden scabbards wrapped with black morocco (Illus. 1104).

For lower ranks as well as officers, **pistols** are to be worn in a holder [*chushka*] attached to the swordbelt, in back and on the left side.

But pistols, as well as the holder, lanyard, and case, are worn only in full dress. Lower ranks' **horse furniture** is to be arranged as follows: valise and horsecloth behind the saddle, the latter being put under the valise and together with it held to the saddle by three black straps with brass double-sided buckles of the previous pattern; the greatcoat, in front of the saddle, is held to it by three identical straps with buckles; along with this, the rolling of the greatcoat and the packing of other items, as well as all articles of uniform, equipment, and armament for the regiment not mentioned here, including the covers for the headdress, are to be unchanged [36].

2 January 1844 - Officers' forage caps are to have a metal **cockade** in front on the capband, as was established at this same time for officers' forage caps in the regular forces (Illus. 1105) [37].

20 May 1844 - With the general fixing of **forage cap** colors for organizations under the War Department, including some changes from previous usage, the forage caps in the Ataman HIS IMPERIAL HIGHNESS THE HEIR AND TSESAREVICH'S Regiment are directed to be light-blue with dark-blue bands and piping around the top that is dark blue for lower ranks and light blue for officers (Illus. 1105) [38].

14 April 1845 - The regiment's former summer uniforms [*letnie mundiry*], or jackets, are replaced by parade [*paradnyi*] **chekmens** of the same color which are to be worn only on holidays and during HIGHEST reviews [*v prazdnichnye dni i pri Vysochaishikh smotrakh*] [39].

27 April 1845 - Consequent to the changes of 14 April 1845 in the dress of the Ataman HIS IMPERIAL HIGHNESS THE HEIR AND TSESAREVICH'S Regiment, this regiment is to have:

1.) *For lower ranks* — **parade coat** [*paradnyi mundir*], in length to reach to 3 1/2 inches above the knee, with pairs of lace bars of white tape [*bason*] on the collar and cuffs; **everyday coat** [*vsednevnyi mundir*], cut like the former winter chekmen but in length to reach to 3 1/2 inches above the knee; **shapka headdress** of black astrakhan, 8 inches high, without an indentation, with a bag of light-blue cloth under which is sewn an oilskin base, and with the current plate and badge for distinction; **ammunition pouch** for 20 rounds in rows, of black, lacquered leather, on a white deerskin belt; **pistol** on a lanyard of light-blue wool, with a case [*chekhol*] of light-blue cloth sewn into a leather holder [*chushka*] that is fixed to the swordbelt on the left side (Illus. 1106, 1107, and 1108).

2.) *For officers* — **parade coat** of light-blue cloth, reaching to 3 1/2 inches above the knee, with pairs of silver lace bars on the collar and cuffs (Illus. 1109); **everyday coat** patterned after the old winter chekmen, but reaching to 3 1/2 inches above the knee; **shapka** of black astrakhan, 8 inches high, without an indentation, with a bag of light-blue cloth, under which is sewn an oilskin base, and with the current plate and badge for distinction; **pistol case** [*chekhol*] of light-blue cloth trimmed wth silver galloon run through with a dark-blue light, and sewn into a leather holder [*chushka*] attached to the swordbelt as for lower ranks.

The **undress chekmen** [*vitse-chekmen*, literally "vice-chekmen"] for officers, the **sharavary pants** for officers and lower ranks, and all items of uniform and armament not mentioned here, as well as **horse furniture**, remain unchanged [40].

18 January 1848 - The pattern for officers' **cartridge-pouches** [*lyadunki*] is confirmed in place of ammunition pouches [*patrontashi*] (Illus. 1110) [41].

5 March 1850 - **Bandoliers for standards** [*pantalery dlya shtandartov*] are to be 4 1/2 inches wide and 56 inches long, lined on the outside with light-blue velvet [*barkhat*] with silver fringes, galloon, and hook, and on the inside with light-blue cloth [42].

15 January 1851 - It is directed that: a.) the **shoulder sling** [*pogonnyi remen*] for the musket is to be made of two unfinished straps blackened on one side, held together with a brass buckle, and fixed to the musket by rings through the stock (Illus. 1111); b.) the **musket case** [*ruzheinye chekhol*] is to be of black Russian leather, lined with grey cloth, and with an unfinished strap around the cock; c.) the copper **kettle** [*kotelok*] is to be carried on the right side of the valise instead of the left, in order to avoid damage to the musket and shashka; d.) officers are not to have holsters [*olstredi*] but rather carry their pistols in a **holder** [*chushka*] of the current pattern; and e.) when lower ranks are going out on **guard duty** [*pri vstuplenii v karauly*], they are to have the musket over the shoulder [43].

18 February 1854 - Officers of Guards Cossack units are to have: a **valise**, exactly like the light cavalry's, attached to the back arch of the saddle, and a case exactly like the guard cuirassiers', 30 inches long and 6 inches in diameter at the bottom end. The case with the **greatcoat** is to be fastened to the front of the saddle with three straps in the same way as soldiers' greatcoats are fastened to cossack saddles [44].

Notes to the Illustrations By Mark Conrad

1093. The uniform of this *uryadnik* (cossack non-commissioned officer) is entirely dark blue except for sky-blue piping, pants stripe, and lace bars. The epaulettes appear to be also sky blue. The bag on the headdress is also sky-blue. This NCO has rank lace on the collar and cuffs, plus the black hourglass shape below the white pompon. The saddle-cloth is dark blue trimmed with white around the outer edge and around the seat. In back of the saddle are (from top to bottom) a grey horse-cloth, dark grey-blue valise, and a white bag.

1094. Dark-blue uniform trimmed with sky-blue. White girdle.

1095. Sky-blue jacket, no piping. Dark-blue pants without stripes.

1096. On the left, a dark-blue chekmen trimmed in sky blue. The badge on the pouch belt is a crowned and wreathed Y (Cyrillic N) over a Roman numeral I. On the right, a sky-blue jacket.

1097. Sky-blue collar and shoulder straps, white gloves.

1098. The main figure wears the dark-blue uniform while the seated cossack has the sky-blue jacket and the oilskin cover to the headdress.

1099. Sky-blue jacket and dark-blue pants. Sky-blue saddle-cloth extensively trimmed with white; the strap holding down the seat is black.

1100. The uniform is all dark blue except for sky-blue piping on the collar and cuffs. The forage cap is sky blue, including the piping on the crown, with a dark-blue band.

1101. Sky-blue jacket.

1103. Sky-blue collar and shoulder straps.

1104. Sky-blue jacket and (seated) dark-blue chekmen.

1105. Sky-blue patch on collar; forage cap with dark-blue band and sky-blue crown. The non-commissioned officer wears the sky-blue jacket and sky-blue forage cap with dark-blue band and piping.

1106. On the left, the dark-blue chekmen; on the right, the sky-blue chekmen. The sky-blue chekmen has no piping, but the black neckcloth can be seen above the collar.

1107. Black pouch on a white belt.

1108. Grey horse. Sky-blue chekmen with white musicians' lace with thin red center stripes. Dark-blue pants. White trumpet cord.

1109. Sky-blue chekmen.

1111. Sky-blue chekmen.

c) *Life-Guards Cossack Regiment [Leib-Gvardii Kazachii polk].*

1 January 1827 - In order to distinguish ranks, officers' **epaulettes** are to have small forged and stamped stars as was laid down at this time for regular forces [45].

17 August 1829 - **Epaulettes** for officers' uniforms are to have a scaled field like the pattern of epaulettes in the light cavalry. The same epaulettes, except made of red copper [*krasnaya med*] with a red cloth backing [*podboi*] and orange wool braid and fringes [*vitok i bakhrama*] are to be issued to the regiment's lower ranks (Illus. 1112 and 1113) [46].

26 May 1835 - By the Administrative Decree confirmed by HIGHEST AUTHORITY governing the Don Host, lower ranks of the Life-Guards Cossack Regiment are prescribed the same dress, armament, and horse equipment as they had previous to this Decree, namely: **Shapka headdress** of black astrakhan, with a scarlet cloth bag; yellow cords and pompons; black **neckcloth**; **chekmen** of dark-blue cloth; scarlet cloth **jacket** [*kurtka*]; lace bars of yellow tape on the chekmen and jacket; **sharavary pants** of dark-blue cloth; white linen **girdle**; grey cloth **greatcoat** with red patches on the collar; **boots** with iron spurs; scaled brass **epaulettes** with yellow wool fringes; **cartridge-pouch** [*lyadunka*] of black lacquered leather, with a brass plate; white deerskin **crossbelt** for the cartridge-pouch; red leather **swordbelt**; standard cossack **saddle** with sweat-cloth and flap; saddle-seat of scarlet cloth, trimmed with white lace; saddle-cloth [*valtrap*] of scarlet cloth, trimmed with white lace; valise of dark grey-blue cloth; horse-cloth of grey cloth; **crossbelt** with brass and iron fittings; steel **saber** with brass guard and leather swordknot; standard cavalry **pistol**; **lance** [*drotik*] with red shaft; **bridle, harness,** and **breast straps** with brass fittings.

Non-commissioned officers [*unter-ofitsery*], clerks [*pisarya*], and medical apprentices [*lekarskie ucheniki*] have silver galloon on their uniform collar and cuffs, as distinct from privates [*ryadovye*].

Generals and field and company-grade officers wear silver lace bars on collars and cuffs, as well as other silver generals' and officers' appointments.

For everyday use, all ranks have a dark-blue cloth **forage cap** with trim and piping as on the collar, as well as black oilskin **covers** for the shapka when in the field [47].

28 October 1836 - The **everyday chekmen** without embroidery introduced on this date for the Don Host and described above is also prescribed for officers of the Life-Guards Cossack Regiment but entirely in dark blue without any piping (Illus. 1114) [48].

15 January 1837 - **Girdles** are not to be worn with the everyday chekmen without embroidery that was established on 28 October 1836 (Illus. 1114). Along with this, it is permitted to use the **chekmen** when authorized and during the summer when officers of the Life-Guards Cossack Regiment would be in red jackets [49].

15 July 1837 - Officers are given a new pattern **sash** of narrow silver lace with three stripes of light-orange and black silk, as established at this time for regular forces [50].

17 December 1837 - A fourth, narrow twist of cord is added to officers' **epaulettes** as in the regular forces [51].

29 April 1838 - The Life-Guards Cossack Regiment is directed to have:

1.) *For lower ranks* — **Shapka headdresses** without cords, with a white tin plate (as in the Life-Guards Lithuania Regiment); iron **epaulettes** without a fringe, with a base of scarlet cloth; **ammunition pouches** [*patrontashi*] (instead of cartridge-pouches [*lyadunki*]) for 40 rounds, of black Russian leather, a similar cover, and a deerskin crossbelt without any appointments; **pistols** of the pattern used in the light cavalry; **pistol holders** [*chushki*] or **cases** [*kobury*] (instead of holsters [*olstredi*]) of polished black leather; orange wool pistol lanyards; the upper part of the **pistol cases** [*chekhly*] up to the lock is of scarlet cloth while the lower part is of shiny black leather; **swordbelts** of red Russian leather; **shashkas** (instead of sabers) with brass hilts, mounts, rings, and endpieces, in wooden scabbards wrapped in black leather (Illus. 1115)

2.) *For officers* — **Shapkas** without cords, with the same appointments as for lower ranks but in silver; **ammunition pouch** (instead of a cartridge-pouch) for 20 rounds, of scarlet morocco, with a cover of scarlet cloth and a crossbelt of silver lace without any colored light and backed with scarlet morocco; **pistols** of the pattern used by officers of light cavalry; **pistol holders** of scarlet morocco; silver pistol lanyards; the upper part of the **pistol case** is of scarlet cloth while the lower part is of scarlet morocco; **swordbelts** of silver lace without any colored stripes, lined with scarlet morocco; **shashkas** (instead of sabers) with gilt hilt, mounts, rings, and endpieces, in wooden scabbards wrapped in black morocco (Illus. 1116).

For officers as well as lower ranks **pistols** are to be carried in a holder attached to the swordbelt on the left side and toward the rear; however, pistols, and likewise the holder, lanyard, and case, are only to be worn in full dress [*polnaya forma*].

Lower ranks' **horse furniture** [*vyuki*] is to be arranged as follows: behind the saddle are the valise and horse-cloth; the latter is put under the valise and together with it tied to the saddle by three black straps with brass two-sided buckles of the previous pattern; the greatcoat is fastened to the front of the saddle with three of the same kind of straps with buckles; along with this, the rolling of the greatcoat, the arrangement of other items, as well as all articles of uniform, equipment, and weaponry in the regiment not mentioned here, including the covers for the headdress, remain without change [52].

2 January 1844 - A metal **cockade** is to be worn on the front of the capband of officers' forage caps, as established at this same time for officers' forage caps in regular forces [53].

20 May 1844 - With the general assignment of colors for **forage caps** to organizations under the War Department, with some changes from previously, the Life-Guards Cossack Regiment is prescribed dark-blue forage caps with red bands and piping around the top [54].

14 April 1845 - The former summer coats, or jackets, of the regiment are replaced by **parade chekmens** [*paradnye chekmeny*] of the same color which are to be worn only on holidays [*prazdnichnye dni*] and during Highest reviews [55].

27 April 1845 - Consequent to the 14 April 1845 changes in the uniform of the Life-Guards Cossack Regiment, the regiment is to have:
1.) *For lower ranks* — **summer coat** [*letnyi mundir*] of scarlet cloth, reaching to 3 1/2 inches above the knees, with two bars of orange tape [*bason*] on the collar and cuffs; **winter coat** [*zimnyi mundir*] — of the same pattern as the former winter chekmen but reaching to 3 1/2 inches above the knees; **shapka headdress** of black astrakhan, 8 inches high, without any indentation, with a bag of scarlet cloth backed with an oilskin base, and with the previous plate (Illus. 1117 and 1118); **ammunition pouch** for 20 rounds in two rows, of black lacquered leather, on a white deerskin belt; **pistol** on an orange woollen lanyard, with a case [*chekhol*] of scarlet cloth trimmed with orange woollen tape, sewn into a holder [*chushka*] of black polished leather attached to the swordbelt on the left side.

2.) *For officers* — **summer coat** of scarlet cloth, reaching to 3 1/2 inches above the knees, with two silver lace bars [*petlitsy*] on the collar and cuffs; **winter coat** of the same pattern as the old winter chekmen but reaching to 3 1/2 inches above the knees; **shapka** of black astrakhan, 8 inches high, without any indentation, with a bag of scarlet cloth under which is sewn an oilskin base, and with the previous plate; **pistol case** of scarlet cloth, trimmed with silver lace and sewn into a holder of scarlet morocco, attached to the swordbelt in the same way as for lower ranks (Illus. 1118).

The **undress chekmen** for officers, the **sharavary pants** for both officers and lower ranks, and all other items of dress and armament not mentioned here, as well as horse equipment, remain without change [56].

28 May 1847 - In cancellation of the order of 20 May 1844, **forage caps** are to be of scarlet cloth the same color as the parade coat, with a band and piping around the top edge of dark-blue cloth (Illus. 1119) [57].

1848 January 18 - The pattern for officers' **cartridge-pouches** [*lyadunki*] is confirmed in place of ammunition pouches [*patrontashi*] (Illus. 1120) [58].

5 March 1850 - Bandoliers for standards are to be 4 1/2 inches wide and 56 inches long, lined on the outside with dark-blue velvet with silver fittings, and on the inside with red cloth [59].

15 January 1851 - It is directed that: a) the **shoulder sling** for the musket is to be made of two unfinished straps, blackened on one side and joined together with a brass buckle, and attached to the musket by its ends through the stock. b) The **musket case** is to be of black Russian leather, lined with grey cloth, and with an unfinished strap alongside the hammer. c) A **copper kettle** is to be carried on the right side of the valise. d) Officers are not to have holsters but are to carry their **pistols** in a case of the current pattern, and e.) lower ranks are to have the **musket** over the shoulder when going out on guard duty [60].

Notes to the Illustrations By Mark Conrad

1112. The officer wears a red jacket without any piping and dark-blue pants. The cossack in the background appears to have a dark-blue forage cap with red capband and piping; the shoulder straps and collar patches of the greatcoat are probably red.

1113. Dark-blue chekmen and pants.

1114. Dark-blue undress chekmen and pants. The forage cap is dark blue with a red band and piping.

1115. The cossack on the right wears the dark-blue chekmen. The non-commissioned officer has the red jacket and dark-blue pants. Notice there is only one lace bar on the collar to make room for the NCo rank lace, and that a small part of the red collar shows above the lace.

1116. Dark-blue chekmen.

1117. The non-commissioned officer wears the dark-blue chekmen. The trumpeter has a red chekmen with yellow musicians' tape. His collar is red with gold NCo lace on the top and in front and musicians' tape on the bottom. His forage cap is dark blue trimmed red.

1118. The officer has the red chekmen while the cossack has the dark-blue version.

1119. Red shoulder straps and collar patch. Red forage cap trimmed with dark blue.

1120. Red chekmen, dark-blue sharavary pants.

d.) Don Cossack Horse-Artillery Batteries [*Donskiya Konno-Artilleriiskiya Kazachya batarei*]. (*)

(*Note: Until 6 April 1834 these were called companies [*roty*].)

1 January 1827 - In order to distinguish ranks, officers' **epaulettes** are to have small forged and stamped stars as established at this time for regular forces [61].

10 July 1827 - The shapka headdresses in Don Horse-Artillery companies are to have round **pompons** — of red wool for lower ranks and in silver for officers (Illus. 1121 and 1122) [62].

7 August 1829 - The field on officers' **epaulettes** is to be scaled in the same way as are the epaulettes in the regular light cavalry; lower ranks have their shoulder straps as before [63].

15 November 1829 - Don Horse-Artillery companies are to have **cartridge-pouches** [*podsumki*] of the same pattern as for regular Horse-Artillery troops, namely: black for lower ranks with two brass cannons, an iron attachment to the strap, and a white crossbelt; **swordbelts** [*portupei*] of red Russian leather (Illus. 1123). Officers have **cartridge-pouches** [*lyadunki*] with a silver cover, gilt cannons, and a crossbelt made from gold galloon with silver fittings, and **swordbelts** of similar gold galloon [64].

6 April 1830 - With the raising of the Life-Guards Don Light Horse-Artillery Company [*Leib-Gvardii Donskaya Legkaya Konno-Artil-leriiskaya rota*] from elements of all three Don Horse-Artillery Companies NºNº 1, 2, and 3, and the formation of only two companies numbered NºNº 2 and 3 in place of these three, both of these are prescribed **gold lace bars** on the officers' coats, while the latter, i.e. Company Nº 3, is also prescribed a **badge** for the headdress [*shapka*] in the same color as the buttons on the shoulder straps and epaulettes and with the cut-out inscription "*Za otlichie*" ["For excellence"] (Illus. 1124) [65].

26 May 1835 - With the Administrative Decree confirmed by HIGHEST AUTHORITY for the Don Host, lower ranks of the Don Horse-Artillery batteries are authorized the same dress, armament, and horse equipment as they had before this Decree, namely:

Shapka headdress of black astrakhan, with a bag of scarlet cloth; red cords and pompons; black **neckcloth**; **jacket** [*kurtka*] of dark-green cloth, with a black cloth collar and red cloth piping on the collar, cuffs, and down the front; **sharavary pants** of dark-green cloth, with red trim; red camlet girdle; greatcoat of grey cloth, with a black collar with red patches; **boots** with iron spurs; scaled brass **epaulettes** with a red fringe; **cartridge-pouch** [*lyadunka*] of black lacquered leather, with a brass plate; white **crossbelt** for the cartridge-pouch, of deerskin with an iron fitting; red leather **swordbelt**; standard cossack **saddle** with sweatcloth and cover flap; saddle-seat of dark-green cloth; saddle-cloth of dark-green cloth, trimmed on the edges with yellow woollen tape [*bason*]; **valise** of dark grey-blue cloth; **horse-cloth** of grey cloth; steel **saber** with a brass hilt; standard cavalry **pistol** with a red woollen lanyard; **bridle**, **harness**, and **breast straps** without any ornamentation.

Non-commissioned officers [*uryadniki*] and clerks have gold galloon on the collar and cuffs of the coat, in distinction to private cossacks (bombardiers and cannoniers).

For everyday use, all ranks have a **forage cap** of dark-green cloth with a band and piping as on the collar, and also, on campaign, black oilskin **covers** for the shapka headdress [66].

In regard to the armament for combatant lower ranks, the following is laid down: non-commissioned officers and cossacks in Don Horse-Artillery batteries do not have muskets but must be armed with two **pistols** each in addition to the **saber** or **shashka** [67].

28 October 1836 - The **everyday chekmen** without embroidery, introduced on this date and described above, is also established for officers of Don Horse-Artillery batteries but in dark green with a black cloth collar and with red piping on the collar and cuffs [68].

15 January 1837 - Girdles are not to be worn with the everyday chekmen authorized on 28 October 1836 [69].

24 January 1837 - Saddle-cloths [*valtrapi*] in batteries of the Don Host are to be dark green as before, but trimmed with yellow cloth instead of yellow tape [70].

15 July 1837 - Officers are given a new pattern **sash** with narrow silver lace and three stripes of light-orange and black silk, as established at this same time for regular forces [71].

17 December 1837 - A fourth, thin twist of cord is added to officers' **epaulettes**, as for regular forces [72].

29 April 1838 - Batteries of the Don Host are ordered to have:

1.) *For lower ranks* — **shapka headdresses** of the previous pattern but without cords; **epaulettes** also of the previous pattern but without fringes; **ammunition pouches** (instead of cartridge-pouches) for 20 rounds, of black Russian leather, with a similar cover and a deerskin crossbelt, without any fittings; **pistols** of the pattern used in the light cavalry; **pistol holders or carriers** [*chushki ili kobury*] (instead of holsters [*olstredi*]) of black, polished leather; pistol lanyards of red wool; the upper part of the **pistol case** [*chekhol*] is made of black cloth up to the lock while the lower part is of black, polished leather; **swordbelts** of red Russian leather; **shashkas** (instead of sabers) with brass hilts, mountings, rings, and endpieces, in a wooden scabbard wrapped in black leather; **saddle-cloths** and **saddle-seats**, the same color as the uniform, with a linen lining, trimmed (the former around the edges and the latter around all around on the seam) with dark-red cloth 1 1/2 inches wide, and with lace of the exact same description, 16 1/2 inches long, on the rear corners of the saddle-cloths; **valises** of grey cloth, 25 1/2 inches long and 22 1/2 inches around with a linen lining and four yellow brass buttons with the raised image of the battery's number (Illus. 1125)

2.) *For officers* — **shapkas** of the previous pattern but without cords; **ammunition pouches** (instead of cartridge-pouches) for 20 rounds, of black morocco, a similar cover, and a crossbelt of gold lace without any colored stripes, and lined with black morocco; **pistols** of the pattern used by officers of light cavalry; **pistol holders** [*chushki*] of black morocco; silver pistol lanyards; the top part of the **pistol cases** [*chekhly*] is of black cloth and the lower is of black morocco; **swordbelts** of gold lace, lined with black morocco; **shashkas** (instead of sabers) with gilt hilt, mountings, rings, and endpieces, in wooden scabbards wrapped with black morocco; **saddle-cloths** and **saddle-seats** the same color as the uniform, lined with black calfskin and trimmed (the former on the edges and the latter around on the seam) with gold lace; **valises** of grey cloth, 21 inches long and 15 3/4 inches around, with a leather lining and four gilt buttons with the raised image of the battery's number (Illus. 1126).

For lower ranks as well as officers, **pistols** are to be carried in holders attached to the swordbelt, in back on the left side, but they are to wear them, as well as the holder, lanyard, and cover, only in full dress. **Horse equipment** for lower ranks is to be arranged as follows: behind the saddle are the valise and horse-cloth, the latter being positioned under the valise and together with it held to the saddle with three black straps with two-sided brass buckles of the previous pattern; the greatcoat in front of the saddle is held to it by three of the same straps with buckles; along with this, the method of rolling the greatcoat and the stowing of other items, as well as all articles of uniform, equipment, and weaponry for the regiment [sic — M.C.] not mentioned here, including covers for the shapka headdress, remain unchanged [73].

22 May 1838 - With the decision to have nine batteries numbered № 1 to № 9 inclusive in the Artillery of the Don Host instead of two, batteries №№ 1, 2, and 3 are prescribed **gold lace bars** on officers' uniforms, and batteries №№ 2 and 3 in addition have **badges** on the headdresses with the inscription "*Za otlichie*".

The newly-established *Reserve* Horse-Artillery Batteries №№ 1, 2, 3, and 4 are ordered to have the same uniform and armament as the other Don batteries, without the gold lace bars or badges for distinction on the headdress, but with the Cyrillic letter *R* added to the number on the epaulettes [74].

2 January 1844 - Officers' forage caps are to have a metal **cockade** in front on the cap band, as established at this time for officers' forage caps in the regular forces [75].

20 May 1844 - With the general assignment, with a few changes from before, of colors for **forage caps** in the War Department [*Voennoe vedomstvo,* i.e. the army in general — M.C.], forage caps in the batteries of the Don Host are to be dark green with black cloth bands and red piping around the edges of the band and the top of the cap. For lower ranks, there is additionally the cut-out battery number on the front of the cap band, backed with yellow cloth [76].

14 April 1845 - The former jackets [*kurtki*] in the batteries are replaced with **chekmens**. At the same time, generals and field and company-grade officers are directed to wear **pistols** with lanyards only when in formation [77].

27 April 1845 - Consequent to the uniform changes of 14 April 1845 in the Don Cossack Artillery, the batteries are to have: **chekmen** — cloth, dark green with black collar and cuffs and red edging on the collar and cuffs and down the front — reaching to 7 inches above the knees; **shapka headdress** of black astrakhan, 8 inches high, without an indentation, with a scarlet bag under which is sewn an oilskin base; **pistol case** [*chekhol*] of the old pattern but sewn into a holder [*chushka*] attached to the swordbelt on the left side (Illus. 1127). Other items of uniform and armament, as well as horse furniture, remain without change [78].

Notes to the Illustrations By Mark Conrad

1121. The Don Horse Artillery wore cossack-style uniforms in the same color scheme as regular artillery (dark green, black collar and cuffs; red piping, shoulder straps, pants stripe, headdress cords, etc.; yellow metal appointments).

1122. The saddle-cloth is trimmed with a band of gold lace edged on the outside with a much narrower strip of lace.

1123. The cartridge-pouch is black on a white belt. Notice the yellow "2" on the shoulder straps.

1124. The honorary scroll on the headdress marks Company № 3.

1125. The trim on the saddle-cloth is one wide band edged on the outside with a much narrower strip.

1126. The officer's collar shown here has red piping only on the top and front and not on the bottom.

1127. This is the parade uniform of the Russian artillery charged by the Light Brigade during the Crimean War. On the day of the battle itself, greatcoats and forage caps would be more likely. The greatcoats would presumably be like those of the regular horse artillery.

e.) *Life-Guards Don Light Horse-Artillery Battery [Leib-Gvardii Donskaya Legkaya Konno-Artilleriiskaya batareya].*[*]

(*Note: Called a company [*rota*] until 6 April 1834 .)

6 April 1830 - Upon its establishment, the **Life-Guards Don Light Horse-Artillery Company** is prescribed uniforms of the same pattern and colors as for the other Horse-Artillery companies of the Don Host, which is to say dark green with red piping, with a red bag on the headdress, and with a black collar and cuffs, but of plissé [*plisovyi*] — or velvet [*barkhatnyi*] for officers — and not of cloth. Lower ranks have two bars of yellow guards tape [*dve petlitsy iz zheltago gvardeiskago basona*] on both the collar and cuffs, scaled epaulettes of red copper-brass [*krasnaya med*] with a cloth lining, woollen fringe, and small cross-strap, all in red, and sharavary pants without stripes. Officers' embroidery on the collar and cuffs and in general all items of uniform and weaponry in the company are to be as in the Guards Horse Artillery (Illus. 1128 and 1129) [79].

23 February 1834 - The **saddle-cloths** [*valtrapy*] for the Life-Guards Don Light Horse-Artillery Company are to be of the same pattern as for the Life-Guards Cossack Regiment but dark green, trimmed with yellow tape [*bason*], with red piping, and with yellow monograms and crowns in the corners. **Saddle-seats** [*podushki na sedla*] are also dark green and have the same tape as the saddle-cloth. For officers the saddle-cloths and seats are the same color and pattern but with gold galloon and silver St.-Andrew's stars on the corners (Illus. 1130 and 1131) [80].

9 December 1834 - Lower ranks of the battery, as well as officers, are to have **saddle-cloths** [*valtrapy*] without stars or monograms, after the example of the Life-Guards Cossack Regiment (Illus. 1132) [81].

26 May 1835 - By the Administrative Decree confirmed by HIGHEST AUTHORITY for the of the Don Host, lower ranks' uniforms, weapons, and horse furniture in the Life-Guards Don Light Horse-Artillery Battery are prescribed to be the same as they had before this Decree, namely:

Shapka of black astrakhan, with a bag of scarlet cloth; red cords and pompons; black **neckcloth**; **chekmen** and **jacket** [*kurtka*] of dark-green cloth, with black plissé collar and red piping on the collar and cuffs; yellow lace bars [*petlitsy*] on the chekmen jacket; **sharavary pants** of dark-green cloth; red camlet **girdle** [*kushak krasnyi, kamlotovyi*], grey cloth **greatcoat** [*shinel*], with a black collar and grey tabs; **boots** with iron spurs; brass **epaulettes**, scaled, with red fringes; **cartridge-pouch** [*lyadunka*] of black lacquered leather, with a brass plate; white **belt** for the cartridge-pouch, of deerskin with an iron fitting; red leather **swordbelt**; standard cossack **saddle**, with sweat-cloth and cover; **saddle-seat** of dark-green cloth, with yellow tape; dark-green cloth **saddle-cloth**, trimmed with yellow tape on the edges; dark blue-grey cloth **valise**; grey cloth **horse-cloth**; **saber** with brass hilt and leather swordknot; standard cavalry **pistol** with a red woollen lanyard; **bridle**, **harness**, and **breast straps** with brass fittings.

Fireworkers [*feierverkery*, this being the title of artillery sergeants — M.C.] and clerks, unlike private cossacks (bombardiers and cannoniers) [*v otmenu ot ryadovykh kazakov (bombardirov i kanonirov)*], have gold galloon on their uniform collars and cuffs.

For everyday use, all ranks have **forage caps** of dark-green cloth, with trim and piping [*vykladka i vypushka*] as on the collar. When on campaign, they have **covers** for the shapka headdress, of black oilskin [82].

28 October 1836 - The **everyday chekmen** [*vsednevnyi chekmen*], without embroidery, introduced on this date in the Don Host and described above, is also instituted for officers of the Life-Guards Don Light Horse-Artillery Battery, except being dark green with a black velvet collar and red piping on the collar and cuffs (Illus. 1133) [83].

15 January 1837 - It is directed that **girdles** [*kushaki*] are not to be worn with the everyday chekmen without embroidery introduced on 28 October 1836 (Illus. 1133) [84].

15 July 1837 - Officers are given a new pattern **sash** [*sharf*] with narrow silver braid [*tesma*] with three rows of light-orange and black silk, as established at this same time for regular forces [85].

17 December 1837 - A fourth, thin twist of braid is added to officers' **epaulettes** just as in the regular forces [86].

29 April 1838 - The battery is ordered to have:

1.) *For lower ranks* — **shapka headdresses** without cords, with a brass plate as prescribed for the Guards Artillery; **epaulettes** as before but without a fringe; **ammunition-pouches** [*patrontashi*] instead of cartridge-pouches [*lyadunki*], for 20 rounds, of black Russian leather, with a similar cover, and with a deerskin belt, without any decoration; **pistols** of the pattern used by light cavalry; **pistol holders or carriers** (instead of holsters) of black polished leather; pistol **lanyards** of red wool; the upper part of the **pistol cases**, up to the lock, are of black cloth, while the lower part is of black polished leather; **swordbelts** of red Russian leather; **shashkas** (instead of sabers) with brass hilt, fittings, rings, and end piece, in a wooden scabbard wrapped in black leather (Illus. 1134).

2.) *For officers* — **shapkas** without cords, with the same plate as lower ranks but gilded; **ammunition-pouches** (instead of cartridge-pouches) for 20 rounds, of black morocco, with a black velvet cover and a gold lace belt lined with black morocco; **pistols** of the pattern used by officers of light cavalry; **pistol holders** of black morocco; silver pistol **lanyards**; the upper part of the **pistol case** is black velvet and the lower part is black morocco; **swordbelts** of gold lace lined with black morocco; **shashkas** (instead of sabers) with hilt, scabbard, and other fittings as for the pattern prescribed at this same time for the L.-Gds. Cossack Regiment (Illus. 1135); the manner of carrying **pistols** and fitting the lower ranks' **horse furniture** in the battery is also as prescribed. Other uniform items and weaponry not mentioned here remain without change [87].

2 January 1844 - Officers' forage caps are to have a metal **cockade** in front on the capband, as established at this time for officers' forage caps in regular forces [88].

20 May 1844 - In the general allocation of **forage-cap** colors for organizations under the War Department, with some changes from formerly, the L.-Gds. Don Light Horse-Artillery Battery is to have dark-green caps with black bands, velvet for officers and plissé for lower ranks, with red piping around the edges of the band and the top of the cap [89].

14 April 1845 - The former jackets [*kurtki*] in the battery are abolished, leaving only the **chekmen** for holidays as well as everyday wear. Along with this officers are ordered to wear **pistols** with lanyards only when in formation [90].

27 April 1845 - Consequent to the 14 April 1845 abolition of the jacket, the battery is ordered to have:

1.) *For lower ranks* — **coat** [*mundir*] like the former winter coat [*zimnyi mundir*], except reaching to 3 1/2 inches above the knee, and a **jacket** [*kurtka*] for use in barracks, like the waistcoats [*leibniki*] of the Guards Horse Artillery but with hooks instead of buttons; **shapka** of black astrakhan, 7 inches high, without an indentation, with a scalet cloth bag under which is an oilskin base, and with the previous plate; **ammunition-pouch** [*patrontash*] for 20 rounds in two rows, of black lacquered leather, on a white deerskin belt; **pistol** with a red woollen lanyard and a black cloth case trimmed with orange woollen tape and sewn into a holder of black polished leather attached to the swordbelt on the left side (Illus. 1136).

2.) *For officers* — **coat** like the former winter coat but reaching to 3 1/2 inches above the knee; **shapka** of black astrakhan, 7 inches high, with a scalet cloth bag, under which is an oilskin base, and the previous plate; **pistol** of the previous pattern but sewn into a holder attached to the swordbelt exactly as for lower ranks (Illus. 1137).

The officers' undress chekmen, sharavary pants of officers and lower ranks, and all other items of uniform and armament not mentioned here, as well as horse furniture, remain unchanged [91].

19 May 1847 - The pattern for the lower ranks' **forage caps** is confirmed: color of the cap — dark green; cap band — black plissé with red piping around both edges; piping around the top of the cap — red [92].

18 January 1848 - The pattern for the officers' **cartridge-pouch** [*lyadunka*] is confirmed in place of the ammunition-pouch [*patrontash*]. All ranks in the battery are directed to have red stripes on their **sharavary pants** for parade and walking-out dress [*pre paradnoi i gorodskoi forme*], as established for the L.-Gds. Horse Artillery (Illus. 1138), while for campaign dress, as before, sharavary without stripes are worn [93].

7 November 1849 - **Pompons** are prescribed to have a circumference of 9 1/6 inches [94].

13 August 1854 - For uniformity, non-combatant lower ranks are to have the same pattern of **shoulder straps** [*pogony*] on the chekmen as non-combatants in the Life-Guards Horse Artillery [95].

Notes to the Illustrations By Mark Conrad

1128. The pompons and cords on the headdress are red, as the girdle also appears to be.

1129. Officers' collars and cuffs have the same special embroidery as the rest of the Guards Horse Artillery.

1130. The outside edge of the saddle-cloth has one wide yellow stripe and then a narrower one outside it. Three black straps hold a grey horse-cloth on top of the dark blue-grey valise. Next to them is a white bag. The private's girdle is apparently white.

1131. Notice the St.-Andrew's stars on the extensively trimmed saddle-cloth. The cords on the officer's shapka appear to be gold.

1132. The private's greatcoat has shoulder straps which appear to be red and apparently a black collar trimmed with red piping and a grey tab. Buttons would be yellow brass.

1136. The musicians' tape is yellow with a red center stripe. There is red piping around the collar, down the front of the chekmen, on the cuffs, and under the swallows' nests. The trumpeter has NCO lace on the collar and cuffs.

1138. There are two wide red stripes and one narrow red stripe on the pants, separated by dark green.

f.) *Generals in the standard general-officers' uniform; General-Adjutants, Aides-de-Camp, and Generals of HIS IMPERIAL MAJESTY'S Suite; Field-grade Duty Officers, Senior and Generals' Adjutants, Assistants to Adjutants and Officials serving in the Internal Administration of the Don Host.*
[U Generalov pri obshchem generalskom mundire, General i Fligel-Adyutantov i Generalov Svity EGO IMPERATORSKAGO VELICHESTVA, Dezhurnykh Shtab-Ofitserov, Starshikh i Generalskikh Adyutantov, Adyutantskikh Pomoshchnikov i Chinovnikov sluzhashchikh po Vnutrennemu Upravleniyu Donskago Voiska.]

28 October 1836 - The **everyday chekmen** without embroidery introduced in the Don Host on this date and described above is also established for those officers of this Host who hold the position of **Aide-de-Camp to HIS IMPERIAL MAJESTY** [*Fligel-Adyutant EGO IMPERATORSKAGO VELICHESTVA*, from German *Flügel-Adjutant* — M.C.], but in dark green with a red collar and white piping on the collar and cuffs (Illus. 1139) [96].

2 January 1837 - The **standard general-officers' coat** [*obshchii generalskii mundir*] is to be of dark-green cloth instead of dark-blue, with the standard generals' embroidery in gold instead of silver. Trousers [*bryuki*], also of dark-green cloth, are prescribed to be worn with this coat, with red piping on the side seams (Illus. 1140). With this uniform it is prescribed to use a **bearskin shabraque** [*valtrap medvezhyago mekha*] with St.-Andrew's stars and a dark-green cloth surcingle [*trok*], as prescribed for generals in the regular forces but in the established cossack pattern (Illus. 1141). **General-Adjutants** [*General-Adyutanty*], as well as as **Generals of HIS MAJESTY'S Suite** [*Generaly Svity EGO VELICHESTVA*] and **Aides-de-Camp**, who are distinguished in uniform from their counterparts in the regular forces by the pattern of their clothing which they have in the Don style, also use the **shabraque** prescribed for these ranks in the regular forces but in the cossack pattern (Illus. 1142, 1143, and 1144) [99].

16 January 1837 - Field and company-grade officers of the Don Host who hold the position of **Field-grade Duty Officer** or **Adjutant** [*Dezhurnyi Shtab-Ofitser ili Adyutant*, from French *de jour* — M.C.], whether it be in a headquarters or duty office [*v Shtabakh i Dezhurstvakh*] or in assignment to a General, are to wear the **uniform** normally prescribed in the Army for Field-grade Duty Officers and Adjutants, i.e. of dark-green cloth with a red collar, red cuff-flaps, and silver lace bars on the collar and cuff-flaps, but of the pattern established for Cossack hosts (Illus. 1145). Those officers in the Life-Guards Cossack Regiment have a silver edging to the collar, cuff-flaps, and cuffs, after the example of Guards Field-grade Duty Officers and Adjutants (Illus. 1146) [100]. They are also prescribed **shabraques** patterned after those used by Field-grade Duty Officers and Adjutants in the Army, but cut in the cossack style and with none having stars (Illus. 1146) [101].

17 February 1837 - Generals of the Don Host who have been released from service before 2 January of this year of 1837 and who have the right to wear the **general-officers' coat** in retirement [*v otstavke*], are to wear this not in the new pattern of dark-green cloth with gold embroidery, but rather in the previous pattern, i.e. of dark-blue cloth with silver embroidery (102).

2 March 1837 - **Generals** are to wear red **girdles** [*kushaki*] with the standard general-officers' coat (Illus. 1140), while **General-Adjutants** and **Aides-de-Camp** in the coats prescribed for their ranks are to wear a white one (Illus. 1142). With the standard cossack coat, though, the girdles prescribed for the host continue to be worn (103).

2 January 1844 - All officers in the positions and ranks named in this section are to have a metal **cockade** on the cap band of the forage cap, identical with that established at this same time for officers of regular forces (Illus. 1147) (104).

30 November 1844 - **Assistants to Adjutants of the Host Duty Office and Regional Duty Offices** [*pomoshchniki Adyutantov Voiskovago i Okruzhnykh Dezhurstv*] are prescribed the Cossack **uniform** for Adjutants but without the aiguillette and with red piping instead of white (Illus. 1148) (105).

31 January 1846 - **Cossack host Officials** [*Chinovniki Kazachikh voisk*] serving in the internal administration of the hosts, except for Adjutants and their Assistants, are to have a **uniform** according to the appended description, along with which:

1) This uniform is to be used by officials in the internal service [*vnutrennyaya sluzhba*] of each cossack host, keeping the same headdress as prescribed for that host.

2) This uniform is only to be worn by those Officials on active duty who are assigned to internal service in the host's own territory, and it is neither for the personnel in detachments permanently detailed away from the host nor for reserve officers entering on internal service who continue to wear the previous uniform.

3) When cossack officers on internal service pass into the reserve, they are not to use this newly authorized uniform, but rather the standard cossack uniform on the previous basis.

Description of Uniform.

Chekmen — of dark-green cloth; red collar with black piping around the edges; green flaps on the cuffs; red piping on the cuffs, cuff-flaps, and down the front from the collar to the bottom of the chekmen's skirts; silver lace bars on the collar and cuff-flaps, of the pattern for Adjutants in Cossack hosts.

Sharavary pants — dark-green with red piping.

Epaulettes — silver.

Sash and shapka headdress — of the former patterns confirmed by HIGHEST AUTHORITY (Illus. 1149) (106).

7 August 1849 - **Generals** of Cossack hosts, when wearing general-officers' coats, are to have **plates** [*gerby*] on the shapka headdress in accordance with the branch of forces to which they belong, i.e. guards or army, and are not to wear tassels [*kutasy*] with the plates (Illus. 1150) (107).

8 February 1850 - **Field-grade Duty Officers and officials on special assignment** [*Dezhurnye Shtab-Ofitsery i chinovniki osobykh poruchenii*], who are prescribed the same uniform as Adjutants, are to have **shapka plates** after the example of Generals and Adjutants of the hosts: of the standard guards pattern for those in the Guards, and of the standard army pattern for others. Tassels are not to be worn with headdress plates (Illus. 1151) (108).

Notes to the Illustrations By Mark Conrad

1139. Dark-green coat and pants; red collar piped white; white piping on the front of the coat and on the dark-green cuffs; red piping on the pants; dark-green forage cap with a red band and three rows of white piping; the visor appears to have lace on the edge, but that is probably just due to the way the artist depicts the reflection of light; silver epaulettes and aiguillette.

1140. Dark-green uniform. The collar, cuffs, cuff-flaps, and piping are red with gold oak-leaf embroidery. The bag on the shapka is also red. The plume is white over a darker color, maybe red but possibly mixed orange and black. The girdle is red.

1141. Black bearskin. The gold stars have a dark double-headed eagle in the center surrounded by a dark ring with a light-colored wreath.

1142. These general officers wear dark-green coats. The collars, cuff-flaps, and bags to the shapkas are red, as may be the bottom half of the plumes. The general's cuffs, edged with gold lace, appear to be dark green. Piping and girdles are white, except for the piping on the pants which is red. Cords, tassels, and embroidery are gold.

1143. A creamy white shabraque with gold lace and stars. The band between the double rows of lace and the thin outside piping to the shabraque are red. The surcingle over the seat is white but the stirrup strap and flap are black. The center of the St.-Andrew's star is a crowned Cyrillic N.

1144. A black sheepskin shabraque with red trim and a silver star. Black surcingle, flap, and stirrup strap.

1145. Dark-green coat and pants. Piping on the collar, cuffs, cuff-flaps, and coat is white. Red collar and cuff-flaps; dark-green cuffs. Apparently, red piping on the pants. Silver appointments.

1146. The same shabraque as in Illustration 1143 but with silver lace and stars, with a dark blue-grey valise with black straps. Dark-green uniform with red collar, cuff-flaps, and shapka bag; white piping on the coat, collar, cuffs, and cuff-flaps; red piping on the pants; dark-green cuffs; silver appointments. Silver lace on the top and front of the collar and on the cuffs and cuff-flaps.

1147. As for Illustration 1139, but definitely no edging on the visor and gold appointments instead of silver.

1148. Dark-green uniform. Red collar, cuff-flaps and shapka bag. All piping is red. Silver appointments.

1149. As described in the text, with dark-green cuffs and cuff-flaps and a red bag on the shapka. Silver appointments.

1150. As for Illustration 1140: dark green, red, and gold.

1151. Dark-green uniform; silver appointments; red collar and cuff-flaps; dark-green cuffs; white piping on the coat. The piping on the pants appears to be either red or white. The shield on the headdress plate appears to be smooth without any device.

II. THE BLACK SEA COSSACK HOST [CHERNOMORSKOE KAZACHE VOISKO].
a.) Horse and foot regiments [Konnye i peshie polki].

1 January 1827 - In order to distinguish rank, officers' **epaulettes** are to have small forged and stamped stars, as established at this time for regular troops [109].

7 August 1827 - All regiments of the Black Sea Host are to have round **pompons** on their shapka headdresses, of white wool for lower ranks and silver for officers (Illus. 1152 and 1153) [110].

7 August 1829 - **Epaulettes** on officers' uniforms are to have scaled fields, like the epaulettes in the regular Light Cavalry [111].

April 1831 - Officers without permanent commissions (za-uryad-ofitsery] are to have small forged and stamped stars on their **epaulettes**, like those established on 1 January 1827 to distinguish ranks [112].

1835 - The Black Sea Host, which has kept the previous **muskets** (the same pattern as that introduced on 29 April 1838 in the Don Host and worn in the same way as in that host, i.e. in back on a black strap across the right shoulder) and **pistol lanyards**, are to have the latter in wool and in two colors — black and yellow — instead of just yellow (Illus. 1154) [113].

29 April 1838 - The changes promulgated this day for the **uniform and armament** of the Don Cossack regiments, described above, apply in equal measure to the regiments of the Black Sea Host, who in regard to horse furniture as well as uniform and armament are to conform to the example of the Don Cossack regiments with the exception of their prescribed distinctions in colors and cuffs (Illus. 1155 and 1156) [114].

1 November 1840 and 1 February 1841 - HIGHEST AUTHORITY confirms the following description of the uniforms and weapons for the Black Sea Cossack Host:

A.) HORSE REGIMENTS [KONNYE POLKI]:
a.) For cossacks:

Shapka headdress — of red cloth; round on top, quilted wadding [steganyi na vate], brim of shaggy black "kurpei" [of uncertain meaning, possibly connected with the Persian "gurbe", meaning a kind of wild cat — M.C.], black chinstrap, silk lace.

Neckcloth [Galstukh] — black cotton.

Coat [Mundir] — dark-blue caftan [kaftan], without a collar, fastened with small hooks from the cartridge-holders [patroniki] on the chest down to the belt; sleeves without cuffs, with the edges trimmed with narrow dark-blue lace [uzkaya sinyaya tesma].

Cartridge-holders on the breast of the coat [Nagrudnyi patronnik na mundire] — black leather, trimmed all around with wide (narrow on the bottom) blue worsted lace; cartridge tubes [napatroniki] for 16 cartridges, of white tin, on thin blue cords [sinie shnurki], pierced by such cords and fastened to the caftan.

Shoulder straps [Pogony] — on a base of blue cloth, of red cloth with the No of the regiment cut out and backed by yellow cloth, with the same regimental No on the buttons.

Belt [Poyas] — of black polished leather, 1 1/3 inches wide, with a double iron clasp and a small iron buckle, endpiece, and loop.

Akhaluk — of red shalloon [*shalonovyi*], quilted with wadding; collar also red, closed with small hooks, of cloth without lace bars.

Sharavary pants — of dark-blue cloth with leather instep straps [*stremenki*].

Boots [*Sapogi*] — of black leather, without spurs, which are replaced by the traditional cossack whip [*nagaika*].

Ammunition-pouch [*Patrontash*] — of black Russian leather, for 24 cartridges; belt 1 1/3 inches wide, black, of undressed leather.

Kinzhal dagger — with a white bone handle; sheath of black leather with iron mountings; worn on the belt on a black strap 1 1/3 inches wide.

Pistol [*Pistolet*] — standard cavalry model.

Holder for carrying the pistol [*Chushka, dlya vkadyvaniya pistoleta*] — of black polished leather, worn on the back of the belt.

Pistol case [*Chekhol pistoletnyi*] — top part of red cloth, trimmed at the closure with narrow worsted blue lace, and the bottom part of black polished leather; trimmed where the leather joins with the cloth and on the end with identical lace; bound with a blue woollen cord with a tassel.

Pistol lanyard [*Shnur pistoletnyi*] — blue, woollen.

Musket and **shoulder sling for the musket** [*Ruzhe i pogonnyi remen k ruzhyu*] — as confirmed by HIGHEST AUTHORITY on 29 April 1838.

Case for the musket [*Chekhol na ruzhe*] — of shaggy black felt [*chernaya kosmataya burka*], with a unfinished black shoulder strap 1 inch wide.

Shashka sword — as confirmed by HIGHEST AUTHORITY on 29 April 1838.

Swordbelt [*Portupeya*] — two carrying slings [*portupeinye remni*] made from straps of polished black leather 1 1/3 inches wide, sewn to the belt; two brass buckles for the slings.

Nagaika — standard cossack whip, braided from rawhide straps (Illus. 1157, 1158, 1159, and 1160).

b.) *For non-commissioned officers* [*uryadniki*]:

Shapka — as for cossacks except that the top is lined all around with standard silver army galloon and crossed over the top with two strips of the same narrow silver galloon.

Coat and **akhaluk** — the same as for cossacks except that the ends of the coat sleeves and the collar of the akhaluk are trimmed around with standard silver army galloon.

Neckcloth, shoulder straps, belt, sharavary, and all other items of uniform and equipment are exactly the same as for cossacks.

c.) *For officers:*

Shapka — red cloth; round top of quilted wadding, trimmed around with wide silver lace and crossed with four strips of narrow silver lace; brim of shaggy black *kurpei*; chinstrap of black silk lace [*shelkovaya tesma*].

Neckcloth — black silk.

Coat — dark-blue caftan, with a collar, trimmed around with narrow silver lace; closed with small hooks from the cartridge-holders on the chest down to the belt; silver lace-bars on the cuffs, which are trimmed with red edging.

Cartridge-holders [*patronnik*] on the breast of the coat — black velvet with encircled with wide — and on the black morocco bottom lids with narrow — silver lace; cartridge-tubes [*napatronniki*] of royal birch [*korelskaya bereza*] for 12 cartridges, in silver mountings with similar small chains fastened to the caftan.

Epaulettes — scaled silver, with a similar field, and the regimental № on the buttons.

Belt — of silver lace 1 1/3 inches wide, backed with black morocco, with silver small and double buckles, endpiece, and loop.

Akhaluk — red stamin cloth [*stamednyi*], quilted with wadding; red cloth collar with silver lace-bars, fastened with small hooks; trimmed with narrow silver lace below the collar and down the front to the belt.

Sharavary — dark-blue cloth with small instep straps and a single row of silver lace.

Boots — of black leather, without spurs, which are replaced by the standard cossack nagaika.

Kinzhal — Circassian [*Cherkesskii*], in silver mountings, worn on the belt on an unfinished black strap, 1 1/3 inches wide and trimmed on the edges with narrow silver lace.

Pistol — standard cavalry model.

Holder for the pistol — of black morocco, worn in back on the belt.

Pistol case — the top part of red cloth, trimmed at the opening with narrow silver lace, the bottom of black morocco, with the part where the leather and cloth meet trimmed with similar lace; tied with a red silk cord.

Pistol lanyard — silver.

Shashka — as confirmed by HIGHEST AUTHORITY on 29 April 1838.

Swordknot — standard cavalry pattern.

Swordbelt — of the standard silver lace for swordbelts, 1/2 inch wide, backed with black morocco, with silver fittings; worn over the shoulder (Illus. 1161, 1162, and 1163).

Nagaika — standard cossack pattern, braided from a rawhide strap.

The wide silver lace on the shapka and on the cartridge-holder is 1/2 inch wide, while the narrow lace on the shapka, around the caftan, on the bottom lids of the cartridge-tubes, on the akhaluk, and on the morocco of the kinzhal is 1/3 inch wide.

B.) FOOT REGIMENTS [*PESHIYE POLKI*]:

a.) *For cossacks:*

Coat [*mundir*] — a jacket [*kurtka*] of dark-blue cloth; the collar closed with small hooks and lined with red edging; the cuffs with the same edging.

Sharavary pants — of dark-blue cloth, without the small instep straps.

Kinzhal dagger — instead of a kinzhal, a bayonet is worn in a standard leather bayonet scabbard hanging from the belt in the same way as the kinzhal in horse regiments.

Musket — standard infantry pattern, with bayonet, also prescribed for non-commissioned officers.

Shoulder sling — for the musket, an unfinished black strap 3/4 inch wide with fittings as in Dragoon regiments.

Frizzen protector [*polunagalishche*] and its **cover** [*chekhol*] — according to the standard infantry pattern.

Knapsack — of calfskin, closed with three iron buckles, on a black crossbelt of unfinished leather 1 1/3 inches wide, worn over the right shoulder.

The shapka headdress, neckcloth, shoulder straps, belt, and all other items of uniform and armament are as in horse regiments, with the exception of the akhaluk, pistol, shashka, swordbelt, and nagaika whip, which are not prescribed for foot regiments (Illus. 1164).

b.) *For non-commissioned officers [uryadniki]:*

Uniforms and weapons are exactly the same as for cossacks, with the only difference being that the **shapka** is trimmed on top with standard silver army galloon and crossed over the top with two strips of the same narrow silver gallon, and that the **coat's** collar and cuffs on the sleeves are trimmed with the same silver army galloon (Illus. 1164).

c.) *For officers:*

Coat — dark-blue jacket [*kurtka*]; silver lace-bars on the collar, which is closed with small hooks and lined with red edging; cuffs on the sleeves also have the edging and lace bars.

Epaulettes — silver, on a red cloth field and with the regimental number on the buttons.

Sharavary — dark-blue cloth, with a single row of silver lace, without instep straps.

Shashka — of the pattern used by the horse regiments, worn on the belt.

Swordknot — standard infantry pattern.

Swordbelt — two lace strips of the standard swordbelt galloon, lined with black morocco, and sewn onto the belt.

The shapka, neckcloth, belt, and all other items of uniform and weaponry are exactly the same as laid down for officers of the horse regiments, except for the akhaluk and nagaika which are not prescribed for officers of foot regiments (Illus. 1165) [115].

1 July 1842 - In accordance with the Administrative Decree [*Polozhenie*] for the Black Sea Cossack Host confirmed on this day by HIGHEST AUTHORITY , the host, which is directed to have twelve horse regiments and nine foot battalions, is prescribed the same uniforms, equipment, weaponry, and other items as were laid down on 1 November 1840 and 1 February 1841, with only the following additions and changes:

A.) HORSE REGIMENTS:

a.) *For cossacks:*

Forage cap (*furazhka*) — of the standard pattern, of dark-blue cloth, with a red cap band and red edging on top around the crown, without a visor.

Greatcoat — of grey cloth, with a similar collar closed with small hooks; of the standard military pattern with linen lining in the shoulders and sleeves; tabs on the collar of red cloth; red cloth shoulder straps on a grey cloth backing, with the regimental number cut out and backed by yellow cloth; the front opening, shoulder straps, and back belt are fastened with tin buttons with the regimental number (Illus. 1166).

Lance [*Pika*] — of the existing pattern, but only to be used in suitable and necessary circumstances.

b.) *For non-commissioned officers:*

The same items are added as for cossacks.

c.) *For trumpeters:*

Coat — the same as for cossacks but the caftan's skirts, breast, and upper half of the sleeves are trimmed with white lace with a red light.

Akhaluk — the same pattern as for other lower ranks but with trim [*vykladki*] around the collar, from the collar to the end of the skirt, and on both sides of the breast, of the same lace as on the coat.

Trumpet — brass, hanging behind the back on a woollen cord [*shnurka*] over the left shoulder.

All other items of uniform and armament are in all ways similar to those of other lower ranks, except for the ammunition-carrier, musket, and lance, which are not prescribed for trumpeters (Illus. 1167).

d.) *For officers:*

Forage cap — the same as for lower ranks but with a visor of lacquered black leather.

Chekmen — of dark-blue cloth; collar of the same cloth, with a red edging around it; the collar and front down to the belt are closed with small hooks. The cut of the chekmen in the back and skirts is in the Circassian style, and the straight sleeves are also in that style.

Cartridge-holder on the breast of the chekmen — exactly the same as on the coat.

Sharavary pants for the chekmen — patterned after the coat's but without stripes or lace.

Greatcoat — of grey cloth; silver-plated buttons with the № of the regiment; a red cloth collar with tabs of the same cloth and a button, lined with grey cloth, while the cape is of grey cloth and 28 inches long, lined with silk or cotton in the same color as the greatcoat.

Chekmens are used in those situations when other forces would wear frock coats. With the chekmen are worn the shashka, belt, swordbelt, and kinzhal (Illus. 1168).

B.) FOOT BATTALIONS:

a.) *For cossacks:*

Forage cap and **greatcoat** — of the same pattern as for horse regiments, except that the greatcoat's collar tabs and shoulder straps and the forage cap's band are of dark-blue cloth instead of red; shoulder straps and buttons on the greatcoat and coat have the battalion number (Illus. 1169).

b.) *For non-commissioned officers:*

The same as for cossacks.

c.) *For drummers:*

Coat — the same jacket as for other lower ranks, trimmed with white lace on the chest, sleeves, back, and swallows' nests, according to the usual pattern for drummers.

Pistol, holder in which to put the pistol, pistol cover, pistol lanyard, and **kinzhal** — according to the patterns for lower ranks of horse regiments.

All other items of uniform and armament are as for lower ranks of foot battalions, except for the cartridge-holders on the chest, the ammunition-carrier, and the musket, which are not prescribed for drummers (Illus. 1169).

d.) *For officers:*

Forage cap, chekmen, cartridge-holders on the breast of the chekmen, sharavary pants for the chekmen, and **greatcoat** — as for horse regiments, but the sharavary have no instep straps, and the greatcoat collar with its tabs as well as the band of the forage cap are of dark-blue cloth, not red [116].

2 January 1844 - Officers' forage caps are to have a metallic **cockade** in front on the cap band, as established at this time for officers' forage caps in the regular forces [117].

20 May 1844 - With the general regulation, with a few changes from before, of colors for **forage caps** in organizations under the War Department, the Black Sea Cossack Host is to have: for horse regiments blue forage caps with a red cap band and red piping around the top, and for foot battalions blue caps with similarly colored bands and red piping around the top of the cap and the top edge of the band [118].

7 July 1844 - Lower ranks of the Black Sea Cossack Host, on internal duty with the host, are prescribed the following uniform and armament:

Shapka — of red cloth; a round top, quilted with wadding; brim of shaggy black *kurpei*; for non-commissioned officers the top of the shapka is trimmed with silver army-pattern galloon.

Chekmen — of dark-blue cloth, with a similar collar and red piping on the collar and cuffs, similarly colored shoulder straps, without cartridge-holders on the chest.

Sharavary — of grey cloth, with red piping.

Greatcoat, **swordbelt**, **ammunition-carrier**, **belt**, **shashka**, and **musket** — as confirmed by HIGHEST AUTHORITY on 1 July 1842 in the description of the uniform and weapons of lower ranks in horse regiments of the Black Sea Cossack Host. **Saddle** — of the pattern used in horse regiments but without the cloth shabraque. The saddle is only for mounted lower ranks (Illus. 1170) [119].

30 November 1844 - Officers are permitted to use **chekmens** not only in those situations where the frock coat would be worn, but also when the undress coat [*vitse-mundir*] would be worn. With this it is directed that the shashka, belt, swordbelt, and kinzhal be worn with these chekmens, and when in the field the pistol with lanyard, too [120].

14 April 1845 - Officers are ordered to wear **pistols** with lanyards only when in formation [121].

4 October 1847 - In the Black Sea Cossack foot battalions it is ordered that Battalion Commanders, Battalion Adjutants, and Majors [*Voiskovye Starshiny*], who in accordance with § 28 of the Regulation for the infantry drill and service of these battalions are required to be in front and mounted, are to have their **saddles** with shabraques [*chepraki*] and other fittings in accordance with the patterns used by the horse regiments of the Black Sea Cossack Host, so that the uniforms and arms of officers in both regiments and battalions are the same [122].

19 October 1847 - Officers of cossack foot battalions are directed to carry **shashkas** of the pattern used by horse regiments, on a swordbelt over the shoulder. With this it is permitted to use lace of local manufacture in the Asiatic style but adapted to the confirmed pattern [123].

26 March 1848 - The uniforms and armament of Black Sea Cossack foot battalions are directed to have the following changes:

1.) **Coat**. Instead of the previous jacket, the chekmen is introduced, like the chekmen of horse regiments of the Black Sea Cossack Host but shorter so that the skirts are about 9 inches from the knees. The collar and cuffs have red piping, with officers additionally having silver lace-bars (Illus. 1171 and 1172).

2.) The **cartridge-holder** on the breast of the coat and chekmen is to be of the previous pattern but sewn on lower than formerly, namely about 7 inches from the bottom of the collar. For lower ranks each side is to have only six cartridge-tubes instead of eight (Illus. 1171 and 1172), so that the straps of the knapsack do not lie on top of them and press into the chest.

3.) The **ammunition-carrier** [*patrontash*] remains the same as before but with 28 cartridges instead of 24, on a crossbelt 1 3/4 inches wide.

4.) The **greatcoat** for lower ranks is of the previous infantry pattern but with red shoulder straps instead of dark-blue, as on the chekmen (Illus. 1171).

5.) Infantry flintlock **muskets** are to be converted to percussion.

6.) On the **musket sling** the case for flints [*ognivnyi chekhol*] is abolished, while a firing-cap pouch [*kapsyulnaya sumka*] for firing caps is fixed to the belt, with 40 firing caps for each cossack. For *plastuny* [light cossack infantrymen — M.C.] armed with rifles [*shtutsery*], this pouch is to made according to the pattern for Rifle battalions, while for other cossacks it is to be the usual infantry pattern. For safeguarding spare firing caps, a tin box is to be issued, as established for infantry.

7.) The **knapsack** is to maintain the previous dimensions but be according to the infantry pattern, and is to be fixed to two straps 1 3/4 inches wide, which are to cross over the chest and be fastened as is usual in the infantry. Under the cover, on the outside back part of the knapsack, a pocket for storing the firing-cap box is to be made. The knapsack has a sheet-iron pot [*kotelok listovago zheleza*] strapped to it where the mess tin goes, and under the cover — the greatcoat rolled in the infantry manner. The strap for fastening the pot is to be 7/8 inch wide and for the greatcoat 1 1/3 inches wide.

8.) Instead of the previous belt, officers are given a **swordbelt** of the pattern for horse regiments, worn over the shoulder (Illus. 1171).

9.) Instead of the silver lace trim on the shapka, cartridge-holders on the chest, and pistol case, as well as for the stripes on the sharavary worn with the coat, for the belt, and for the swordbelt, it is permitted to use **galloon** locally manufactured in the Asiatic style. This galloon must have a black silk light [*protsvet*] on the sides and a gold light down the middle. For the belt its width is 1 1/3 inches; for the swordbelt, pistol cover, sharavary stripes, and around the base of the shapka and around the cartridge-holders on the chest it is 1 inch wide; and on the bottoms of the cartridges-holders, along the cross-seams of the crown of the shapka, and for the kinzhal strap it is 1/2 inch wide.

10.) The **saddle** and **shabraque** of Battalion Commanders, Majors, and Battalion Adjutants, which up to now had no definite pattern, are to be of the pattern for horse regiments of the Black Sea Host (Illus. 1171) [124].

22 August 1848 - With the issue of conical bullets [*puli konicheskoi formy*] for the rifles of plastuny in foot battalions, it is permitted to widen the cartridge-tubes on the chest so that the space in which the bullet is to be placed is commensurate with their size [125].

16 January 1850 - The **pistol** prescribed for musicians of the Black Sea Host's foot battalions is ordered to be worn in a holder [*kobura*] on the waistbelt on the left hip. For this, two loops (of black leather, 1 1/3 inches wide), are sewn onto the outside of the holder at the top on the right side, straight and equidistant from both edges, 1/2 inch apart from each other, large enough so that when put onto the waistbelt they are able to move freely. When placed in the holder, the pistol is to be behind the kinzhal, somewhat askew, with the hammer back and against the skirt, and the butt forward and even with the hilt of the kinzhal [126].

17 June 1850 - The nine foot battalions of Black Sea Cossacks are to begin using linen summer pants such as the infantry have [127].

27 October 1851 - The Black Sea Cossack foot battalions are to have the new model English bugles (Illus. 1173) [128].

Notes to the Illustrations By Mark Conrad

1152. Since 1816 Black Sea Cossack uniforms had been patterned after those of the Don Host. Black shapka, white pompon and cockade, red bag. Dark-blue jacket piped red, notice the sleeves down the back; white cords and tassels; white girdle. Dark-blue pants. Dark-blue shabraque edged with a red stripe; rolled light-grey greatcoat held by black straps to a dark grey-blue valise, next to a white bag.

1153. Like 1152 but silver lace-bars and silver lace on the shabraque.

1155. Silver non-commissioned officers' lace on collar and cuffs.

1157. From top to bottom, a cartridge-tube is white metal, lace, black leather, and lace again. Surrounding the row of tubes on three sides is more lace.

1161. Two rows of silver lace down the front of the akhaluk. The chains from the cartridge-holders attach to metal fixtures on the caftan.

1164. The red shoulder straps have a yellow number 1.

1167. Grey horse. White trumpet cord. Notice how the musician's tape across the chest is both on the caftan and underneath on the akhaluk. Each large row is actually made of a single central tape surrounded by another tape, each white tape having a red light. The white tapes down the center front of the akhaluk have a red light, and run down both sides, separated by red piping. Notice the nagaika whip hanging from the wrist.

1169. Dark-blue forage cap with red piping around the crown. Each row on the drummer's chest is actually two lengths of white tape having a red light. 1173. White summer pants. Black strap for the bugle.

b.) *Life-Guards Black Sea Cossack Battalion [Leib-Gvardii Chernomorskii Kazachii divizion].* [*]

(*Note: Until 1 July 1842 this was called the Life-Guards Black Sear Cossack Squadron [*Leib-Gvardii Chernomorskii Kazachii eskadron*].

1 January 1827 - In order to distinguish rank, officers' **epaulettes** are to have small forged stars, as established at this time in the regular forces [129].

7 August 1829 - **Epaulettes** for officers' uniforms are to be with scaled fields, like the pattern in the regular Light Cavalry. The same epaulettes, except of copper, with red cloth backing and orange woollen cords and fringes, are given to the squadron's lower ranks (Illus. 1174) [130].

29 April 1838 - The changes in **uniform** and **armament** for the Life-Guards Cossack Regiment, put into effect on this date and described above, apply in an equal measure to the Life-Guards Black Sea Squadron, which as its 7th Squadron forms part of the regiment. The only difference is that the squadron retains, as previously, **muskets** with cases when in mounted formation, worn behind the back over the right shoulder, on a black rawhide shoulder belt 1 1/8 inches wide with a brass buckle (Illus. 1175 and 1176) [131].

1 November 1840 and 1 February 1841 - The following description of uniforms and arms for the Life-Guards Black Sea Squadron is confirmed by HIGHEST AUTHORITY:

a.) *For privates:*

Shapka headdress — of red cloth; round top, quilted with wadding, trimmed around with standard orange guards tape [*bason*], and crossed on top with two stripes of the same orange guards tape; brim of shaggy black *kurpei*; chinstrap of black silk lace.

Neckcloth — as before, unchanged.

Coat [*mundir*] — a dark-blue cloth caftan, without a collar, sleeves thrown back, lined with red stamin lining [*stamedovaya podkladka*]; trimmed around and on the pockets with orange guards tape with a black center light and thin red stripes on the sides; fastened 2 1/2 inches from the belt with small hooks; cuffs on the sleeves of black plissé [*plisa*], with guards lace-bars.

Cartridge-holders [*patronniki*] **on the breast of the coat** — black plissé, with similar bottom lids and below them a pocket-patch [*karmanchik*], also of black plissé; cartridge-holders, pocket-patches, and bottom lids trimmed with guards tape; brass cartridge-tubes [*napatronniki*] for 12 cartridges, tinned, on orange woollen cords passed through a similar cord fastened to the caftan.

Shoulder straps — in the hussar style, of orange woollen cord, which hold fast the thrown-back sleeves by means of a tin button with a crest.

Belt — of red Russian leather, 1 1/2 inches wide, trimmed on the edges with orange guards tape, with iron double and small buckles, endpiece, and loop.

Akhaluk — red cloth, to the mid-thigh and 7 inches shorter in length than the caftan, with standard guards lace-bars on the collar and cuffs; trimmed to the end of the skirts with guards tape with red lights; lined with the usual linen lining.

Sharavary — of dark-blue cloth, with leather instep straps [*stremenki*]; trimmed along the sides with two rows of guards tape with a black light down the center and red lights on the sides.

Boots — unchanged except that they are without spurs, which are replaced by the standard cossack nagaika.

Gloves — as before, unchanged.

Ammunition-carrier — of black Russian leather, with a similar cover, for 24 cartridges, according to the pattern confirmed by HIGHEST AUTHORITY on 29 April 1838; its crossbelt is equally in accordance with this pattern.

Kinzhal — with a white bone hilt; sheath mounted in black leather and iron, worn on the belt on a red Russian leather strap 1 1/2 inches wide, trimmed along the sides with tape as on the belt.

Pistol, holder in which to put the pistol, pistol case, pistol lanyard, musket, shoulder sling for the musket, musket case, shashka, and **swordknot** all remain as before without any changes, according to their currently confirmed patterns.

Swordbelt — two red Russian leather swordbelt straps 1 1/2 inches wide, sewn onto the belt; two brass swordbelt buckles as before, with fittings and loops of the same Russian leather.

Small bag for bullets [*Meshochek dlya pul*] — of red Russian leather, the cover trimmed with standard guards tape; worn on the belt (Illus. 1177).

Nagaika — Standard cossack whip, braided from rawhide.

Greatcoat — of grey factory-made army cloth [*fabrichnoe armeiskoe sukno*], with a similar collar closed with small hooks; standard military pattern, with linen lining in the shoulders and sleeves; shoulder straps and collar tabs of red cloth; front opening, shoulder straps, and belt fastened with tinned buttons with a crest.

b.) *For non-commissioned officers [unter-ofitsery]:*

Shapka — exactly the same as for cossacks, but trimmed around the top with wide — and over the top with two strips of narrow — silver galloon, instead of with orange guards tape.

Coat and **akhaluk** — of the patterns for private cossacks' coats and akhaluks, with the only difference being that the coat's cuffs and the akhaluk's collar and cuffs are trimmed with silver galloon; also, instead of two lace-bars of orange guards tape on the akhaluk collar, there is only one lace-bar of this same tape (Illus. 1177).

Neckcloth, shoulder straps, belt, pistol, musket, and all other items of uniform and armament are in all respects similar to the private cossacks' uniforms and armament described above.

c.) *For trumpeters:*

Coat and **akhaluk** — as for the rest of the lower ranks but trimmed in the usual trumpeters' style with wide guards tape with red lights, namely: on the coat — 21 rows on the chest, with the points on one side lined up with the same number and positions of points on the other side; on the sleeves — twice on the whole length of each, indeed diagonally in 17 rows with the points up, and around the cuffs; on the akhaluk — around the collar, from there along the front to the end of skirts; 20 rows on the chest, with the points exactly aligned one side with the other; on the sleeves — twice on the whole length of each, indeed diagonally in 17 rows with the points up, and around the cuffs; swallow's nests on the sleeves are blue cloth with scarlet cloth lining, trimmed around and across (with four rows) with the same tape.

All other items of uniform and armament are of exactly the same patterns as for other lower ranks, excepting the ammunition-carrier and musket, which are not prescribed for trumpeters (Illus. 1178).

The tape around the shapka headdress and on the lace-bars is the standard guards lace-bar tape [*gvardeiskii petlichnyi*],

7/8 inch wide, while on all the rest of the uniform and accouterment items it is of the pattern used for the Life-Guards Crimean-Tatar Squadron, 1/3 inch wide.

For trumpeters holding non-commissioned officer's rank the collar and cuffs are to be trimmed with the silver galloon prescribed for this rank. Besides the tape trim described above, tape also covers the coat's and akhaluk's seams on both sides of the back and down its center from the collar to the belt, in one row (Illus. 1178).

d.) *For officers:*

Shapka - of red cloth: round top, quilted with wadding, trimmed around with wide silver lace [*tesma*], and crossed with four strips of narrow silver lace; brim of shaggy black *kurpei*; chinstrap of black silk lace; the same shapka is also for the undress coat [vitse-mundir].

Neckcloth — as before, unchanged.

Coat — a caftan of dark-blue cloth, without a collar, with thrown-back sleeves; trimmed around and on the pockets with wide silver lace; fastened with small hooks 2 1/2 inches from the belt; black velvet cuffs on the sleeves, with silver lace-bars; dark-blue stamin lining under the coat, but scarlet-red silk in the sleeves.

Cartridge-holders on the breast of the coat — black velvet, with similar bottom lids and pockets beneath them; trimmed around with one row — and above the pockets with two rows — of wide silver lace; the lower part of the cartridge-holder and below the pocket — trimmed with narrow lace; cartridge-tubes for 10 cartridges, of royal birch, in silver mountings, with similar small chains fixed to the caftan. All this is also on the undress coat, but without the pocket-patches.

Epaulettes — scaled silver, with a similar field, backed with red cloth, the guards crest on the buttons; underneath the epaulettes are shoulder straps in the hussar style.

Belt — of silver lace 1 1/3 inches wide, lined with red morocco, with a silver buckle, endpiece, and loop; the same for the undress coat.

Akhaluk — red cloth, reaching to mid-thigh, with standard guards lace-bars on the collar and cuffs; fastened down to the belt with small hooks; trimmed to the end of the skirts with narrow silver lace; lined with red stamin; but with the undress coat it is black silk, quilted with wadding.

Undress coat [*vitse-mundir*] — a caftan of dark-blue cloth, with a similar collar which is closed with small hooks, as is the front opening down to the belt; the cut of this caftan in the back and skirts is in the Circassian style, as are the straight sleeves.

Sharavary — of dark-blue cloth, with leather instep straps, having along the sides two rows of wide silver galloon with a light, but for the undress coat of dark-blue cloth without lace.

Boots — unchanged, except without spurs, their function being fulfilled by the standard cossack nagaika.

Gloves — as before, unchanged.

Kinzhal — Circassian, in silver mountings; worn from the belt on a red morocco strap 1 1/3 inches wide, trimmed on the edges with narrow silver lace; the same kinzhal is to be worn with the undress coat.

The **pistol**, **holder in which to put the pistol**, **pistol case**, **pistol lanyard**, **shashska**, and **swordknot** remain as before, without any changes, in accordance with their currently confirmed patterns.

Swordbelt — of standard silver swordbelt lace 1 inch wide, lined with red morocco, with silver fittings; worn over the shoulder; for the undress coat the same.

Nagaika — standard cossack whip, braided from a rawhide strap (Illus. 1179 and 1180).

Greatcoat — of grey cloth; standard officers' pattern, with silver buttons with crests; a proportionally sized collar of red cloth, lined with grey cloth, and a cape 28 inches long as measured from the bottom edge of the collar.

On all items the wide **lace** is 1 1/3 inches wide while the narrow is 1/2 inch.

The undress coat and the accouterments prescribed for it form the **usual everyday officers' uniform** [*vsednevnaya, obyknovennaya ofitserskaya forma*] in all those situations in which the undress coat is worn in other regiments which have them. The combination of pistol and lanyard with this dress forms the officers' **full campaign uniform** [*polnaya pokhodnaya forma*] when these gentlemen officers are wearing the sash with the undress coat.

With weapons, this squadron's complete parade uniform for officers forms their **full parade uniform** [*polnaya paradnaya forma*]. This uniform combination, without the pistol and its lanyard, forms the **officers' holiday uniform** [*prazdnichnaya ofitserskaya forma*] [132].

8 May 1841 - In the Life-Guards Black Sea Cossack Squadron the lining of officers' **coats** is to be of red stamin instead of blue [133].

12 March 1842 - Officers are to wear **coats** on the same basis as chekmens are used in the Life-Guards Cossack Regiment [133].

1 July 1842 - By the Administrative Decree concerning the Black Sea Cossack Host, confirmed on this date by HIGHEST AUTHORITY , the Life-Guards Black Sea Battalion is prescribed the same items of uniform, equipment, armament, and so on as were laid down on 1 November 1840 and 1 February 1841, with only the following additions and changes:

a.) *For privates:*

Forage caps — standard pattern, of red cloth, with a blue cap band, without a visor.

Lance — according to the current pattern, used only in suitable and necessary circumstances.

b.) *For non-commissioned officers and trumpeters:*

Except for the lance, which is not authorized for these ranks, changes are in accordance with those for the rest of the lower ranks.

c.) *For officers:*

Forage cap — exactly the same as for lower ranks but with a peak of lacquered black leather.

Coat — according to the previous pattern, but lined underneath with red stamin instead of dark-blue.

Undress coat — replaced by the chekmen, which has the exact same form as the previous caftan used as the undress coat.

Cartridge-holders on the breast of the chekmen — as on the coat but for 12 cartridges, and also differing from that previously on the undress coat in that there are velvet pockets under the bottom lids.

Akhaluk — black silk, quilted with wadding, worn with the undress coat — not authorized with the chekmen.

Chekmens are worn in those situations where other troops would wear frock coats. With the chekmen are worn: shapka, belt, swordbelt, shashka, and kinzhal [135].

2 January 1844 - Officers' forage caps are to have a metallic **cockade** on the front of the cap band, as was established at this time for officers' forage caps in the regular forces [136].

20 May 1844 - With the general regulation of forage-cap colors, with some changes from before, for organizations and units under the War Department, the Life-Guards Black Sea Cossack Battalion is directed to have red **forage caps** with a dark-blue cap band and piping around the top (Illus. 1181) [137].

30 November 1844 - Officers are permitted to use **chekmens** with silver lace-bars on the collar and cuffs not only in those circumstances where frock coats [*syurtuki*] would be worn, but also when undress coats [*vitse-mundiry*] are worn. Also, with these chekmens the shashka, belt, swordbelt, and kinzhal are to be worn, and when on campaign the lanyard with pistol, too [138].

14 April 1845 - The **coats** [*mundiry*] currently in the Life-Guards Black Sea Battalion are to be used only in holiday uniform. For normal use lower ranks are to have blue **chekmens** patterned after the officers' undress coats [*vitse-mundiry*], but without epaulettes (Illus. 1182).

Together with this, it is laid down that officers are to carry **pistols** with lanyards only when in formation [139].

27 April 1845 - HIGHEST AUTHORITY confirms the following descriptions of several uniform items for the Life-Guards Black Sea Battalion:

a.) *For lower ranks:*

Parade coat [*paradnyi mundir*]: the outer [*verkhnii*] coat — of scarlet cloth, without a collar, with thrown-back sleeves, with lace-bars of standard guards tape with a light; the pattern is exactly the same as used up to now in blue cloth; the under [*nizhnii*] coat or akhaluk — of blue cloth, with lace-bars of standard guards tape with a light, according to the pattern used up to now in scarlet cloth; cartridge-holders on the chest of black plissé, also according to the previous pattern; coats are trimmed with guards pattern tape with a light the color of the cloth; for the two items the height above the knee is: 3 1/2 inches for the first, and 7 inches for the second. Epaulettes are not authorized for lower ranks (Illus. 1183).

Everyday coat [*vsednevnyi mundir*] — completely in accordance with the pattern now in use, except that it is 3 1/2 inches above the knees.

Sharavary pants — for the parade coat they remain without change, while for the everyday coat they have no lace.

Ammunition-carrier — according to the pattern of the Life-Guards Cossack Regiment, for 20 cartridges in two rows, of black lacquered leather, on a white deerskin belt.

b.) *For officers:*

Parade coat — as for lower ranks except that the lace-bars on the collar and sleeves are silver; tape is replaced by silver galloon, and the cartridge-holders on the chest are black velvet instead of plissé (Illus. 1184).

Everyday coat — exactly like the pattern now in use except that it reaches to 3 1/2 inches above the knees.

Undress chekmen [*vitse-chekmen*] — patterned after the everyday coat, but without lace-bars; reaching to the knees.

Sharavary — remain unchanged when for the parade coat, but without lace when for the everyday coat and undress chekmen [140].

15 January 1851 - It is ordered that:

a.) The **shoulder sling for the musket** be made from two rawhide straps, blackened on one side, joined together by a brass buckle.

b.) The **musket case** be made of black Russian leather and lined with black cloth.

c.) The **copper pot** be worn on the right side of the valise.

d.) Officers not have holsters [*olstredi*], but rather wear **pistols** in a carrier [*chushka*] of the present pattern.

e.) Lower ranks have **muskets** over the shoulder when going out on guard duties [141].

Notes to the Illustrations By Mark Conrad

1174.—Notice that in the guards, private cossacks are called privates (*ryadovye*) instead of cossacks (*kazaki*) as in the line. The uniform at the beginning of Tsar Nicholas I's reign in 1825 was: Metal — silver; headdress — red bag, yellow cords and upper and lower pompons (silver for officers); jacket — dark blue, dark-blue collar, red sleeves and cuffs, dark-blue false sleeves and their cuffs; lace-bars — yellow (silver for officers); epaulettes — yellow (silver for officers); dark-blue pants; white belt; dark-blue shabraque with a red cushion, white trim (silver for officers); trumpeters' lace — yellow with a red light.

1175 and 1176. In contrast to Illustration 1175, in what may be a printing error, Viskovatov here shows red jackets with dark-blue sleeves and red false sleeves. This is unsupported by the text.

1177. In agreement with the text, the caftan with its thrown-back sleeves is dark blue and the akhaluk is red. The non-commissioned officer is called an *unter-ofitser* rather than an *uryadnik* as he would in a line cossack unit.

1178. Grey horse.

1179. The red lining of the false sleeves shows at the shoulders, matching the red sleeves of the akhaluk and contrasting with the dark-blue caftan.

1180. The undress coat.

c.) *Black Sea Cossack Artillery [Chernomorskaya Kazachaya Artilleriya].*

1 January 1827 - In order to distinguish rank, officers' **epaulettes** are to have small forged and stamped stars, as established at this time for regular forces [142].

10 July 1827 - In this Artillery the shapka headdresses are to have round **pompons**, of red wool for lower ranks and silver for officers (Illus. 1185 and 1186) [143].

7 August 1829 - **Epaulettes** for officers' uniforms are to have scaled fields, like the epaulettes in the regular Light Cavalry [144].

25 August 1829 - With the renumbering of the Horse-Artillery Company of the Black Sea Cossack Host from № 6 to № 4, this latter **number** is prescribed for officers' epaulettes and lower ranks' shoulder straps [145].

April 1831 - Officers without permanent positions [*za-uryad-ofitsery*] are to have small forged and stamped stars on their **epaulettes** as established on 1 January 1827 to distinguish rank [146].

29 April 1838 - The changes in **uniform** and **armament** for Don Horse-Artillery batteries, put into effect on this date and described above, are extended in an equal measure to the Artillery of the Black Sea Cossack Host (Illus. 1187) [147].

22 May 1838 - With the renumbering of the Horse-Artillery Battery of the Black Sea Cossack Host from № 4 to № 10, this latter **number** is prescribed for officers' epaulettes and lower ranks' shoulder straps [148].

1 November 1840 and 1 February 1841 - HIGHEST AUTHORITY confirms the following description of uniforms and armament of the Artillery batteries of the Black Sea Cossack Host:

A.) HORSE BATTERIES:

a.) *For cossacks:*

Shapka headdress — of red cloth; round on top, quilted with wadding; brim of shaggy black *kurpei*; chinstrap of black silk lace.

Neckcloth — black cotton.

Coat [*mundir*] — a dark-green caftan, without a collar, trimmed with red edging: sleeves without cuffs; trimmed on the edges with narrow red woollen lace [*tesma*].

Cartridge-holders on the breast of the coat — black leather, trimmed around with wide — and on the bottom lids with narrow — red woollen lace; cartridge-tubes for 16 cartridges, of white tin, on red cords passed through a similar cord fixed to the caftan; the tops of the tin cartridge-holders are brass-mounted.

Shoulder straps — red cloth on a dark-green backing, with the number of the battery cut out and backed by yellow cloth, and with the battery number again on the brass artillery buttons.

Belt — of red morocco, 1 1/3 inches wide, with brass double and small buckles, endpiece, and loop.

Akhaluk — of black demicotton [*demikoton*], quilted and wadded; black cloth collar without lace-bars, trimmed with red edging, closed with small hooks; the bottom of the collar and down the sides of the front to the belt trimmed with narrow woollen lace.

Sharavary — of dark-green cloth, with one row of narrow red lace, and with leather instep straps.

Boots — of black leather, without spurs, which are replaced by the standard cossack nagaika.

Kinzhal — with a white bone hilt; sheath mounted in black leather and iron, worn from the belt on a small strap of red Russian leather, 1 1/3 inches wide.

Pistol — standard cavalry model.

Holder in which to put the pistol — of polished black leather, worn behind on the belt.

Pistol case — the top of black cloth; trimmed at the opening with narrow red woollen lace; the bottom of polished black leather; trimmed where the leather joins the cloth and on the end with the same lace; tied with a red woollen cord with tassel.

Pistol lanyard — red wool.

Shashka — confirmed by HIGHEST AUTHORITY on 19 April 1838.

Swordknot for the shashka — of red Russian leather.

Swordbelt — two swordbelt straps of red Russian leather, 1 1/3 inches wide, sewn onto the belt; two brass swordbelt buckles (Illus. 1188).

Nagaika — standard cossack pattern, braided from a rawhide strap.

b.) *For non-commissioned officers [uryadniki]:*

The uniform and armament of non-commissioned officers is completely the same throughout as the uniform and armament of plain cossacks, with the only difference being that for them the **shapka** is trimmed with gold army galloon around the top and across over the crown, and the same galloon is used to trim the edges of the coat sleeves and around the collar of the akhaluk.

c.) *For trumpeters:*

Coat — of the pattern for the rest of the lower ranks but trimmed in the usual trumpeters' manner with wide white army lace with a red light in the center, and to be exact: around the front opening down to the end of the skirts; on the chest — on one side with 22 rows with points, and on the other with the same number of rows and also with points; on the sleeves — twice down the whole length of each, and indeed diagonally, in 19 rows with the points upward; swallows' nests on the sleeves, of scarlet cloth backed with dark-green cloth and trimmed around and across (four rows) with the same lace.

Akhaluk — of the exact same appearance and cut as described above for other lower ranks, but trimmed with the same lace as on the coat, namely: around the collar, from there along the front to the belt, 21 rows on the chest with the points on one side exactly corresponding to those on the other (Illus. 1189).

Red worsted lace: when wide and on the cartridge-holders on the chest it is 7/8 inch, and when narrow on caftan sleeves and on the bottom lids it is 1/2 inch wide.

For trumpeters holding non-commissioned officer rank the collar and cuffs are to be trimmed with the gold galloon prescribed for this rank, and in addition to the lace trim described above, seams are covered with this lace on both sides of the back and down its center from the collar to the belt, in one row.

d.) *For officers:*

Shapka — of red cloth: round top, quilted with wadding, trimmed around with wide gold lace, and crossed with four strips of narrow gold lace; brim of black *kurpei*; chinstrap of black silk lace.

Neckcloth — black silk.

Coat — dark-green caftan, without a collar, trimmed with red edging and around with narrow gold lace; closed with small hooks from the cartridge-holders on the chest to the belt; the cuffs, with gold lace-bars, are trimmed with red edging.

Cartridge-holders on the breast of the coat — black velvet, trimmed around with wide — and on the black morocco bottom lids with narrow — gold lace; cartridge-tubes for 12 cartridges, of royal birch in a gold mounting, fastened to the caftan with small chains that are also gold.

Epaulettes — scaled gold with a similar field on which is the number or the battery, the artillery buttons also having this number.

Belt — of gold lace 1 1/3 inches wide, lined with black morocco, with gold double and small buckles, endpiece, and loop.

Akhaluk — black silk, quilted with wadding; two gold lace-bars on the collar, which is of black cloth, closed with small hooks, and trimmed with red edging; trimmed with narrow gold lace below the collar and along the sides of the front to the belt.

Sharavary — of dark-green cloth, with leather instep straps and one row of narrow gold lace along the sides.

Boots — of black leather, without spurs, which are replaced by the standard cossack nagaika.

Kinzhal — Circassian, mounted in silver; worn from the belt on a small black rawhide strap, 1 1/3 inches wide, which is lined on the edges with narrow gold lace.

Pistol — standard cavalry model.

Holder in which to put the pistol — of black morocco, worn in back at the belt.

Pistol case — the top part of black cloth, trimmed at the opening with narrow gold lace, and the bottom of black morocco; trimmed with the same lace where the leather joins the cloth and on the end; tied with a red silk cord.

Pistol lanyard — silver.

Shashka — confirmed by HIGHEST AUTHORITY on 29 April 1838.

Swordknot — standard cavalry pattern.

Swordbelt — of standard gold swordbelt lace, 1 inch wide, lined with black morocco, with gold fitting; worn over the shoulder (Illus. 1190).

Nagaika — standard cossack whip, braided from a rawhide strap.

Gold lace: the wide lace on the shapka and cartridge-holders on the chest is 1 inch wide, and the narrow lace around the caftan, on the shapka, the bottom lids of the cartridge-holders, the akhaluk, and on the morocco leather of the kinzhal is 1/2 inch wide.

B.) FOOT BATTERY:

a.) *For cossacks:*

All items of uniform and armament are exactly the same in form and appearance as for the horse batteries, with the exception of the instep straps of the sharavary, the swordknot on the shashka, and the nagaika, which are not prescribed for cossacks of the foot battery.

b.) *For non-commissioned officers:*

The uniform and weapons of non-commissioned officers in the foot battery are the same throughout as the uniform and weapons of non-commissioned officers in horse batteries, with the same exceptions as noted for plain cossacks (Illus. 1191).

c.) *For trumpeters:*

The patterns for trumpeters' uniforms and weapons in this battery are in accordance with those for trumpeters of horse batteries, with the exceptions as for the other lower ranks of this battery.

d.) *For officers:*

All items relating to the uniform and armament of officers of the foot battery are the same as prescribed for officers of horse batteries, with the exception of instep straps on the sharavary and the nagaika, which are not authorized in the foot battery. The swordknot on the shashka, though, is the standard infantry pattern [149].

1 July 1842 - In accordance with the Administrative Decree for the Black Sea Cossack Host, put into effect on this date and confirmed by HIGHEST AUTHORITY, the host, which is to have one Horse-Artillery Brigade consisting of three Horse-Artillery Light Batteries Nº 10, Nº 11, and Nº 12 (i.e. in sequence after the batteries of the Don Host), and one Garrison Artillery Foot Company, is prescribed those same items of uniform, equipment, arms, and so on as were laid down on 1 November 1840 and 1 February 1841, with only the following additions and changes:

A.) HORSE-ARTILLERY BATTERIES:

a.) *For cossacks:*

Forage cap — of the standard pattern, of dark-green cloth, with a black cloth cap band and red edging, without a visor.

Greatcoat — of grey cloth, standard military pattern, with linen lining in the shoulders and sleeves; black cloth collar, lined with grey and trimmed around with red edging, closed with small hooks; red cloth tabs on the collar; red cloth shoulder straps on a grey cloth backing, with the battery number cut out and backed with yellow cloth; brass artillery buttons, with the Nº of the battery, on the tabs, down the front, and on the belt.

b.) *For non-commissioned officers:*

The same additions are made as for cossacks.

c.) *For trumpeters:*
No kinds of additions or changes are made except for those indicated above for other lower ranks.

d.) *For officers:*
Forage cap — the same as for lower ranks but with a peak of black lacquered leather
Chekmen — of dark-green cloth, with a black collar with red piping on it as well as on the sleeves. The cut of the back and skirts of this chekmen is in the Circassian fashion, which is also the style for the straight sleeves.
Cartridge-holders on the breast of the chekmen — the same as on the coat.
Sharavary for the chekmen — also of dark-green cloth, but without stripes or galloon (Illus. 1192).
Greatcoat — of grey cloth; the cape is also of grey cloth, 28 inches long, lined with either silk or cotton cloth the color of the greatcoat; collar of black cloth, lined with grey and trimmed around with red edging; red cloth tabs on the collar; gilded artillery buttons with the No of the battery, on the tabs and down the front.

B.) FOOT GARRISON ARTILLERY COMPANY:
a.) *For cossacks:*
Forage cap — the same as for cossacks of the Horse Artillery batteries.
Greatcoat — as for Horse batteries, but without numbers on the shoulder straps and buttons.

b.) *For non-commissioned officers:*
Changes are the same as for Horse batteries, except that shoulder straps and buttons have no numbers.

c.) *For trumpeters:*
The uniform and armament of trumpeters in the Foot Garrison Artillery Company are exactly the same as in the Horse batteries, but with the changes and additions noted for other lower ranks of this company.

d.) *For officers:*
Forage cap, chekmen, and **cartridge-holders on the chekmen** — of the same patterns as for officers of Horse batteries.
Sharavary for the chekmen — also according to the pattern for Horse batteries, but without the leather instep straps which, like the nagaika, are not authorized for the Foot Garrison Company.
Epaulettes and the buttons on them are without numbers.
Greatcoat — of the same cut and appearance as for Horse batteries, but without numbers on the buttons.

The **chekmen** is used in those situations where other forces would wear frock coats. With chekmens are worn: shapka, belt, swordbelt, shashka, and kinzhal [150].

2 January 1844 - Officers' forage caps are to have a metallic **cockade** on the front of the cap band, as established at this time for officers' forage caps in the regular forces [151].

20 May 1844 - With the general assignment, with some changes from before, of **forage-cap** colors for organizations under the War Department, the Black Sea Cossack Artillery is directed to have them in dark green with a black cloth band and red piping on the band's edges and around the top of the cap, and lower ranks of Horse batteries are additionally to have the No of the battery cut out and backed on yellow cloth [152].

30 November 1844 - Officers are permitted the use of **chekmens** not only in those circumstances where frock coats would be worn, but also when the undress coat [*vitse-mundir*] would be worn. With this it is established that with the chekmen is worn the shashka, belt, swordbelt, and kinzhal, and when on campaign, the lanyard and pistol, too [153].

14 April 1845 - Officers are ordered to wear **pistols** with lanyards only when in formation [154].

12 May 1851 - Summer linen **pants** are ordered to be taken into use in the Foot Garrison Artillery Company of the Black Sea Cossack Host [155].

8 July 1852 - Chekmens in Horse-Artillery batteries of the Black Sea Host are to be made following the example of the Don and Caucasian Cossack Artillery with a red edging down the front [156].

12 February 1852 - In regard to the uniform and armament of such ranks in the Black Sea Cossack Host as Generals, Field-grade Duty Officers, persons on special assignment, Adjutants and Adjutants' Aides, and officers serving in the internal administration, the following changes are directed to be effected:

1.) **Shapka (papakha)** in accordance with the confirmed pattern for the Separate Caucasus Corps.
a.) For Generals when wearing the standard general-officers' parade half-caftan [*obshche-generalskii paradnyi polukaftan*], the top of the shapka is of red cloth with gold general-officers' embroidery along the four seams and lower edge.
b.) For Field-grade Duty Officers, persons holding special assignments, Adjutants and Adjutants' Aides, and officers

serving in the internal administration, the top of the shapka is of dark-green cloth with silver galloon having two narrow stripes down the middle.

2.) All these ranks, except Generals, are to have an **undress half-caftan** [*vitse-polukaftan*] in addition to the parade half-caftan [*paradnyi polukaftan*] of the same pattern as the parade version but without lace-bars on the collar and without flaps on the cuffs. Girdles [*kushaki*] are not authorized for wear with the undress half-caftan.

3.) **Armament**:

a.) For Generals when wearing the standard general-officers' parade half-caftan, instead of the dragoon cavalry saber, it is the pattern confirmed for the Separate Caucasus Corps, on a swordbelt over the shoulder, of gold galloon backed with black morocco. Its fittings are gilt. With the host coat [*voiskovoi mundir*], however, it is the shashka prescribed for the host, on a swordbelt of the pattern approved for it.

b.) For Field-grade Duty Officers, persons on special assignment, Adjutants and Adjutants' Aides, and officers serving in internal administration, instead of the cavalry saber, it is the shashka prescribed for the host to which each person belongs. The shashka is worn over the shoulder on a swordbelt of silver galloon backed with black morocco. The fittings for the swordbelt are silver plated (Illus. 1193) [157].

Apart from the uniform changes described here for units of the Black Sea Host, all the resolutions presented above in article f. covering the Don Host in regard to that host's standard general-officers' dress and its uniforms for General-Adjutants and Aides-de-Camp of HIS IMPERIAL MAJESTY, Field-grade Duty Officers, Senior and General-Adjutants, and Adjutants' Aides, apply in equal measure to the Black Sea Host.

Notes to the Illustrations By Mark Conrad

1185. Since 1816 the Black Sea artillery patterned its uniform after that of the Don Host artillery. Like regular artillery, also, it is dark green with black collar and cuffs, piped red, and red shoulder straps. Red bag on the headdress. Red pistol lanyard. Dark-green shabraque trimmed red.

1186. For officers, gold lace-bars.

1187. White crossbelt for the black ammunition-carrier. Red girdle.

1188. Red tape on the end of the sleeves and down the front of the akhaluk.

1189. The akhaluk has tape down both sides of the front opening, with red piping in between. The tape on the sides of the front of the coat has red piping on the edge. The tape on the skirt has red piping on its outer side. The ends of the sleeves have red trim, and the lace around the cartridge-holders is also red.

1191. This *uryadnik* has gold non-commissioned officers' lace on the collar and ends of the sleeves.

1192. In contrast to the other illustrations, here the tops of the cartridges are definitely round.

1193. Dark-green coat with red collar piped white. Cuffs are dark green with red flaps, piped white. The dark-green pants have red piping. Metal is silver. White aiguillette.

NOTES

(1) Collection of Laws and Directives relating to the Military Administration [*Sobranie Zakon. i Postanovlenii, do chasti Voennago Upravleniya otnosyashchikhsya*], 1827, Book I, pg. 3.

(2) Ibid., Book III, pg. 17.

(3) Ibid., 1829, Book III, pg. 127.

(4) Ibid., 1831, Book II, pg. 33.

(5) Highest confirmed *Polozhenie* for administering the Don Host, 26 May 1835, in a supplement to an order to the Civil Administration, list under letter Z, pgs. 282 and 283.

(6) Highest confirmed *Polozhenie* for administering the Don Host, Part 1, § 169 and notes 170, 171, 172, and 212.

(7) Collection of Laws and Directives, 1836, Book IV, pg. 25.

(8) Ibid., 1837, Book I, pg. 29.

(9) Ibid., Book III, pg. 47.

(10) Ibid., Book IV, pg. 325.

(11) Ibid., 1838, Book II, pgs. 413-422.

(12) Ibid., Book III, pg. 145.

(13) First continuation of the Code of Military Directives [*Svod Voennykh Postanovlenii*], 1841, pgs. 82 and 83, §§.18 and 20, and roster of persons serving in the Don Host.

(14) Correspondence of the Director of the Department of Military Settlements to the Government Ataman [*Nakaznyi Ataman*] of the Don Host, 6 October 1841, № 2548.

(15) Order of the Minister of War, 2 January 1844, № 1.

(16) —— —— —— 20 May 1844, № 69, pg. 24.

(17) Sixth continuation of the Code of Military Directives, 1846, pg. 49.

(18) Order of the Minister of War, 14 April 1845, № 1.

(19) —— —— —— 27 April 1845, № 72.

(20) —— —— —— 29 January 1849, № 9.

(21) —— —— —— 14 September 1849, № 88.

(22) —— —— —— 7 November 1849, № 111.

(23) Collection of Laws and Directives, 1827, Book I, pg. 3.

(24) Ibid., Book III, pg. 17.

(25) Highest confirmed models of jacket, chekmen, and sharavary, located at the Model Storehouse [*Obraztsovyi magazin*] of the Commissariat Department of the War Ministry.

(26) Collection of Laws and Directives, 1829, Book II, pg. 233.

(27) Ibid., Book III, pg. 127, and information received by the Commissariat Department of the War Ministry.

(28) Highest Order.

(29) Information received by the Commissariat Department of the War Ministry.

(30) Information received by the Commissariat Department of the War Ministry.

(31) Highest confirmed *Polozhenie* for administering the Don Host, 26 May 1835, from a supplement to an order to the Civil Administration, list under letter Z, pgs. 282 and 283.

(32) Collection of Laws and Directives, 1836, Book IV, pg. 25.

(33) Ibid., 1837, Book I, pg. 29.

(34) Ibid., 1837, Book III, pg. 47.

(35) Ibid., Book IV, pg. 325.

(36) Ibid., 1838, Book II, pgs. 413-422.

(37) Order of the Minister of War, 2 January 1844, № 1.

(38) Order of the Minister of War, 20 May 1844, № 69, pg. 12..

(39) —— —— —— 14 April 1845, № 66.

(40) —— —— —— 27 April 1845, № 72.

(41) —— —— —— 18 January 1848, № 16.

(42) —— —— —— 5 March 1850, № 18.

(43) —— —— —— 15 January 1851, № 6.

(44) —— —— —— 18 February 1854, № 21.

(45) Collection of Laws and Directives, 1827, Book I, pg. 3.

(46) Ibid., 1829, Book III, pg. 127, and information received from the Commissariat Department of the War Ministry.

(47) Highest confirmed *Polozhenie* for administering the Don Host, 26 May 1835, from a supplement to an order to the Civil Administration, list under letter Z, pgs. 282 and 283.

(48) Collection of Laws and Directives, 1836, Book IV, pg. 25.

(49) Ibid., 1837, Book I, pg. 29.

(50) Ibid., Book III, pg. 47.

(51) Ibid., Book IV, pg. 325.

(52) Ibid., 1838, Book II, pgs. 413-422.

(53) Order of the Minister of War, 2 January 1844, № 1.

(54) ———— ———— ———— 20 May 1844, № 69, pg. 10.

(55) ———— ———— ———— 14 April 1845, № 66.

(56) ———— ———— ———— 27 April 1845, № 72.

(57) ———— ———— ———— 28 May 1847, № 92.

(58) ———— ———— ———— 15 January 1851, № 6.

(59) ———— ———— ———— 5 March 1850, № 18.

(60) ———— ———— ———— 15 January 1851, № 6.

(61) Collection of Laws and Directives, 1827, Book I, pg. 3.

(62) Ibid., Book III, pg. 17.

(63) Ibid., 1829, Book III, pg. 127, and information received at the Commissariat Department of the War Ministry.

(64) Information received at the Commissariat Department of the War Ministry.

(65) Collection of Laws and Directives, 1830, Book II, pgs. 309 and 310.

(66) Highest confirmed *Polozhenie* for administering the Don Host, 26 May 1835, from a supplement to an order to the Civil Administration, Part I, at the end, list under letter Z, pgs. 282 and 283.

(67) *Polozhenie* for administering the Don Host, Part I, § 173.

(68) Collection of Laws and Directives, 1836, Book IV, pg. 25.

(69) Ibid., 1837, Book I, pg. 29.

(70) Ibid., Book I, pg. 365.

(71) Ibid., Book III, pg. 47.

(72) Ibid., Book IV, pg. 325.

(73) Ibid., 1838, Book II, pgs. 413-422.

(74) Correspondence of the Department of Military Settlements, 16 January 1854, № 236, and information received at the Commissariat Department of the War Ministry.

(75) Order of the Minister of War, 2 January 1844, № 1.

(76) ———— ———— ———— 20 May 1844, № 69, pg. 26.

(77) ———— ———— ———— 14 April 1845, № 66.

(78) ———— ———— ———— 27 April 1845, № 72.

(79) Highest confirmed patterns located in the Model Storehouse of the Commissariat Department of the War Ministry.

(80) The same models, and information received at this Department.

(81) Collection of Laws and Directives, 1834, Book IV, pg. 217.

(82) Highest confirmed *Polozhenie* for administering the Don Host, 26 May 1835, in a supplement to an order to the Civil Administration, Part I, at the end, list under letter Z, pgs. 282 and 283.

(83) Collection of Laws and Directives, 1836, Book IV, pg. 25.

(84) Ibid., 1837, Book I, pg. 29.

(85) Ibid., Book III, pg. 47.

(86) Ibid., Book IV, pg. 325.

(87) Ibid., 1838, Book II, pgs. 413-422.

(88) Order of the Minister of War, 2 January 1844, № 1.

(89) ———— ———— ———— 20 May 1844, № 69, pg. 18.

(90) ———— ———— ———— 14 April 1845, № 66.

(91) ———— ———— ———— 27 April 1845, № 72.

(93) ———— ———— ———— 18 January 1848, № 16.

(94) ———— ———— ———— 7 November 1849, № 111.

(95) ———— ———— ———— 13 August 1854, № 81.

(96) Collection of Laws and Directives, 1836, Book IV, pg. 25.

(97) Ibid., 1837, Book I, pg. 3.

(98) Description of the uniforms and weapons of the troops of the Russian IMPERIAL Army, St.-Petersburg, 1845, Book III, pg. 321.

(99) Ibid., pgs. 319-324.

(100) Collection of Laws and Directives, 1837, Book I, pg. 31.

(101) Description of the uniforms and weapons of the troops of the Russian IMPERIAL Army, St.-Petersburg, 1845, Book III, pgs. 325 and 326.

(102) Collection of Laws and Directives, 1837, Book I, pg. 59.

(103) Ibid., pg. 71.

(104) Order of the Minister of War, 2 January 1844, № 1.

(105) Memorandum of the Minister of War to the Government Ataman of the Don Host, 30 November 1844, № 3,938.

(106) Order of the Minister of War, 31 January 1846, № 28.

(107) 7 August 1849, № 71.

(108) 8 February 1850, № 11, and memorandum of the Minister of War to HIS IMPERIAL HIGHNESS THE HEIR AND TSESA-REVICH, Ataman of all the Cossack Hosts, 14 February 1850, № 762.

(109) Collection of Laws and Directives, 1827, Book I, pg. 3.

(110) Ibid., Book III, pg. 17.

(111) Ibid., 1829, Book III, pg. 127.

(112) Ibid., 1831, Book II, pg. 33.

(113) Information received from the Commissariat Department of the War Ministry.

(114) Collection of Laws and Directives, 1838, Book II, pgs. 418-422.

(115) Description, confirmed by HIGHEST AUTHORITY 1 November 1840 and 1 February 1841, of the uniforms and weapons of the Black Sea Cossack Host.

(116) Highest confirmed *Polozhenie* for administering the Black Sea Cossack Host, 1 July 1842, Appendix, pgs. 79-95.

(117) Order of the Minister of War, 2 January 1844, № 1.

(118) 20 May 1844, № 69.

(119) Memorandum of the Minister of War to the Commander of the Separate Caucasus Corps, 7 July 1844, № 2,174.

(120) Ibid., 30 November 1844, № 3,936.

(121) Order of the Minister of War, 14 April 1845, № 66.

(122) Memorandum of the Minister of War to HIS IMPERIAL HIGHNESS the Commander-in-Chief of the Guards and Grenadier Corps, 4 October 1847, № 3,913.

(123) Ibid., 19 October 1847, № 4,107.

(124) Memorandum of the Minister of War to the Commander of the Separate Caucasus Corps, 26 March 1848, № 1,197.

(125) Ibid., 22 August 1848, № 3,577.

(126) Order of the Minister of War, 16 January 1850, № 3.

(127) Memorandum of the Minister of War to the Commander of the Separate Caucasus Corps, 17 July 1850, № 259.

(128) Ibid., 24 October 1851, № 2,442.

(129) Collection of Laws and Directives, 1827, Book I, pg. 3.

(130) Ibid., 1838, Book III, pgs. 127, and information received from the Commissariat Department of the War Ministry.

(131) Collection of Laws and Directives, 1838, Book II, pgs. 413-422.

(132) Description, confirmed by HIGHEST AUTHORITY 1 November 1840 and 1 February 1841, of the uniforms and weapons of the Black Sea Cossack Host.

(133) Correspondence from the Director of the Department of Military Settlements to the Commissariat Department of the War Ministry, 8 May 1841, № 1,212.

(134) Order of the Minister of War, 12 March 1842, № 21.

(135) Description, confirmed by HIGHEST AUTHORITY 1 November 1840 and 1 February 1841, of the uniforms and weapons of the Black Sea Cossack Host, pgs. 67-77.

(136) Order of the Minister of War, 2 January 1844, № 1.

(137) 20 May 1844, № 69.

(138) Memorandum of the Minister of War to the Commander of the Separate Caucasus Corps, 30 November 1844, № 3,936.

(139) Order of the Minister of War, 14 April 1845, № 66.

(140) 27 April 1845, № 72.

(141) 15 January 1851, № 6.

(142) Collection of Laws and Directives, 1827, Book I, pg. 1.

(143) Ibid., Book III, pg. 17.

(144) Ibid., 1829, Book III, pg. 127.

(145) Historical Description of the Clothing and Arms of the Russian Army, Volume XIX, Section II, article 34.

(146) Collection of Laws and Directives, 1831, Book II, pg. 33.

(147) Ibid., 1838, Book II, pgs. 418-422.

(148) Historical Description of the Clothing and Arms of the Russian Army, Volume XIX, Section II, article 34.

(149) Description, confirmed by HIGHEST AUTHORITY 1 November 1840 and 1 February 1841, of the uniforms and weapons of the Black Sea Cossack Host.

(150) Highest confirmed *Polozhenie* for administering the Black Sea Cossack Host, 1 July 1842, Appendix, pgs. 97-103.

(151) Order of the Minister of War, 2 January 1844, № 1.

(152) 20 May 1844, № 69.

(153) Memorandum of the Minister of War to the Commander of the Separate Caucasus Corps, 30 November 1844, № 3,936.

(154) Order of the Minister of War, 14 April 1845, № 66.

(155) Memorandum of the Minister of War to the Commander of the Separate Caucasus Corps, 12 May 1851, № 1,137.

(156) Order of the Minister of War, 8 July 1852, № 75.

(157) 12 February 1852, № 51.

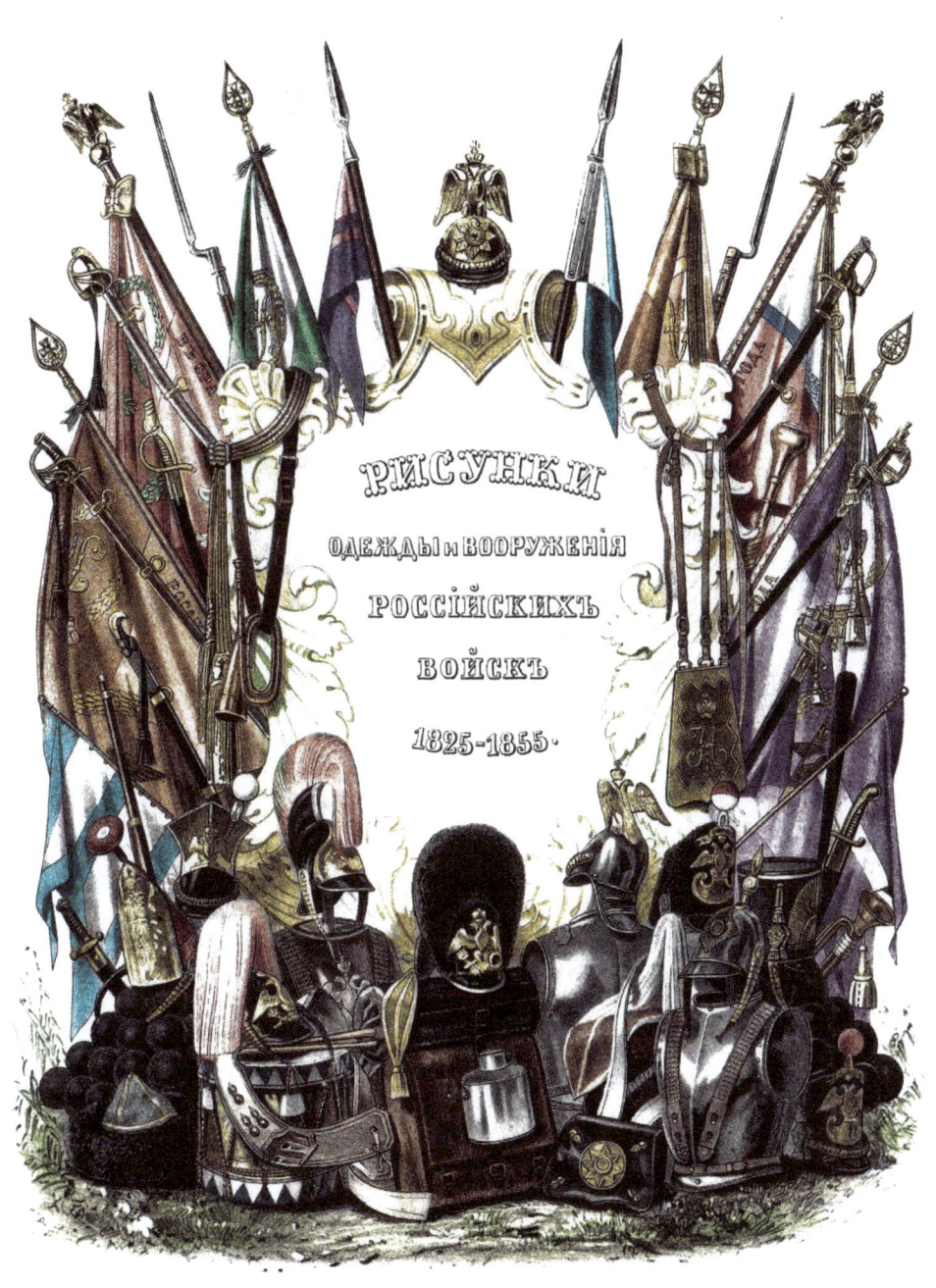

РИСУНКИ

ОДЕЖДЫ и ВООРУЖЕНІЯ

РОССІЙСКИХЪ

ВОЙСКЪ

1825-1855.

PLATES LIST OF ILLUSTRATIONS

1109. Field-grade Officer. The Ataman HIS IMPERIAL HIGHNESS THE HEIR AND TSESAREVICH'S Regiment. 1845-1855.

1110. Officers' Cartridge-pouch for The Ataman HIS IMPERIAL HIGHNESS THE HEIR AND TSESAREVICH'S Regiment, established 18 January 1848.

1111. Private. The Ataman HIS IMPERIAL HIGHNESS THE HEIR AND TSESAREVICH'S Regiment. 1851-1855.

1112. Field-grade Officer. Life-Guards Cossack Regiment. 1829-1838.

1113. Private. Life-Guards Cossack Regiment. 1829-1838.

1114. Field-grade Officer. Life-Guards Cossack Regiment. (In vice-chekmen.) 1836-1844.

1115. Non-commissioned Officer and Private. Life-Guards Cossack Regiment. 1838-1845.

1116. Company-grade Officer. Life-Guards Cossack Regiment. 1838-1845.

1117. Non-commissioned Officer and Trumpeter. Life-Guards Cossack Regiment. 1845-1847.

1118. Private and Field-grade Officer. Life-Guards Cossack Regiment. 1845-1848.

1119. Non-commissioned Officer. Life-Guards Cossack Regiment. 1847-1855.

1120. Field-grade Officer. Life-Guards Cossack Regiment. 1848-1855.

1121. Cossack. Don Cossack Horse-Artillery Companies. 1827-1834.

1122. Company-grade Officer. Don Cossack Horse-Artillery Companies. 1827-1838.

1123. Cossack. Don Cossack Horse-Artillery Companies. 1829-1838.

1124. Company-grade Officer. Don Cossack Horse-Artillery Company № 3. 1830-1838.

1125. Cossack. Don Cossack Horse-Artillery Batteries. 1838-1845.

1126. Company-grade Officers. Don Cossack Horse-Artillery Batteries. 1838-1845.

1127. Cossack. Don Cossack Horse-Artillery Batteries. 1845-1855.

1128. Private. Life-Guards Don Horse-Artillery Company. 1830-1835.

1129. Company-grade Officer. Life-Guards Don Horse-Artillery Company. 1830-1834.

1130. Private. Life-Guards Don Horse-Artillery Battery. 1834.

1131. Company-grade Officer. Life-Guards Don Horse-Artillery Battery. 1834.

1132. Field-grade Officer. Life-Guards Don Horse-Artillery Battery. 1834-1838.

1133. Company-grade Officer. Life-Guards Don Horse-Artillery Battery. 1836-1844.

1134. Private. Life-Guards Don Horse-Artillery Battery. 1838-1845.

1135. Company-grade Officer. Life-Guards Don Horse-Artillery Battery. 1838-1845.

1136. Trumpeter. Life-Guards Don Horse-Artillery Battery. 1845-1855.

1137. Company-grade Officer. Life-Guards Don Horse-Artillery Battery. 1845-1855.

1138. Company-grade Officer. Life-Guards Don Horse-Artillery Battery. 1848-1855.

1139. Aide-de-Camp. Don Host. 1836-1845.

1140. General. Don Host. (In the standard general-officers' uniform.) 1837-1845.

1141. General-officers' Shabraque for the Don Host, established in 1837.

1142. General-Adjutant and General of HIS IMPERIAL MAJESTY'S Suite. Don Host. 1837-1845.

1143. General-Adjutants' Parade Shabraque for the Don Host, established in 1837.

1144. Aides'-de-Camp Campaign Shabraque for the Don Host, established in 1837.

1145. Field-grade Duty Officer. Don Host. 1837-1850.

1146. Adjutant, from the Life-Guards Cossack Regiment. 1837-1850.

1147. General-Adjutant. Don Host. 1844.

1148. Adjutant's Aide, from the Don Host. Host and Regional Duty Offices. 1844-1850.

1149. Field-grade Officer of the Don Host, serving in the Host's Internal Administration. 1846-1850.

1150. General of Guards Cossack units. 1849-1855.

1151. Field-grade Duty Officer. Don Host. 1850-1855.

1152. Cossack. Black Sea Cossack Host. 1827-1835.

1153. Company-grade Officer. Black Sea Cossack Host. 1827-1838.

1154. Cossack. Black Sea Cossack Host. 1835-1838.

1155. Non-commissioned Officer. Black Sea Cossack Host. 1838-1840.

1156. Field-grade Officer. Black Sea Cossack Host. 1838-1840.

1157. Cossack and Non-commissioned Officer. Horse Regiments of the Black Sea Cossack Host. 1840-1855.

1158. Kinzhal for Combatant Lower Ranks of the Black Sea Cossack Host, according to the pattern confirmed 1 November 1840 and 1 February 1841.

1159. Swordbelt for Combatant Lower Ranks of the Black Sea Cossack Host, according to the pattern confirmed 1 November 1840 and 1 February 1841.

1160. Musket Case for Combatant Lower Ranks of the Black Sea Cossack Host, according to the pattern confirmed 1 November 1840 and 1 February 1841.

1161. Company-grade Officer. Horse Regiments of the Black Sea Cossack Host. 1840-1855.

1162. Kinzhal for Officers of the Black Sea Cossack Host, according to the pattern confirmed 1 November 1840 and 1 February 1841.

1163. Swordbelt and Belt for Officers of the Black Sea Cossack Host, according to the pattern confirmed 1 November 1840 and 1 February 1841.

1164. Cossack and Non-commissioned Officer. Foot Battalions of the Black Sea Cossack Host. 1848.

1165. Company-grade Officer. Foot Battalions of the Black Sea Cossack Host. 1840-1848.

1166. Cossack. Horse Regiments of the Black Sea Cossack Host. 1848-1855.

1167. Trumpeter. Horse Regiments of the Black Sea Cossack Host. 1842-1855.

1168. Company-grade Officers. Horse Regiments of the Black Sea Cossack Host. 1842-1844.

1169. Cossack and Drummer. Foot Battalions of the Black Sea Cossack Host. 1842-1848.

1170. Horse Cossack. Black Sea Cossack Host, on Internal Duty. 1844-1855.

1171. Cossack and Field-grade Officer. Foot Battalions of the Black Sea Cossack Host. 1848-1855.

1172. Cossack. Foot Battalions of the Black Sea Cossack Host. 1848-1855.

1173. Bugler. Foot Battalions of the Black Sea Cossack Host. 1854-1855.

1174. Private. Life-Guards Black Sea Cossack Squadron. 1829-1838.

1175. Private. Life-Guards Black Sea Cossack Squadron. 1838-1840.

1176. Company-grade Officer. Life-Guards Black Sea Cossack Squadron. 1838-1840.

1177. Private and Non-commissioned Officer. Life-Guards Black Sea Cossack Squadron. 1840-1845.

1178. Trumpeters. Life-Guards Black Sea Cossack Squadron. 1840-1845.

1179. Company-grade Officer. Life-Guards Black Sea Cossack Squadron. 1840-1845.

1180. Company-grade Officer. Life-Guards Black Sea Cossack Squadron. 1840-1842.

1181. Company-grade Officer. Life-Guards Black Sea Cossack Battalion. 1844-1855.

1182. Non-commissioned Officer. Life-Guards Black Sea Cossack Battalion. 1845-1855.

1183. Private. Life-Guards Black Sea Cossack Battalion. 1840-1845.

1184. Field-grade Officer. Life-Guards Black Sea Cossack Battalion. 1845-1855.

1185. Cossack. Horse-Artillery Company of the Black Sea Cossack Host. 1827-1838.

1186. Company-grade Officer. Horse-Artillery Company of the Black Sea Cossack Host. 1827-1838.

1187. Cossack. Horse-Artillery Battery of the Black Sea Cossack Host. 1838-1840.

1188. Cossack. Horse-Artillery Batteries of the Black Sea Cossack Host. 1840-1845.

1189. Trumpeter. Horse-Artillery Batteries of the Black Sea Cossack Host. 1840-1845.

1190. Company-grade Officer. Horse-Artillery Batteries of the Black Sea Cossack Host. 1840-1845.

1191. Non-commissioned Officer. Foot Garrison Artillery Company of the Black Sea Cossack Host. 1840-1845.

1192. Company-grade Officer. Horse-Artillery Batteries of the Black Sea Cossack Host. 1842-1845.

1193. Adjutant, from the Black Sea Cossack Host. 1851-1855.

Cossack. Don Cossack Regiments. 1827-1838

Company-grade Officer and Non-commissioned Officer [Uryadnik]. Don Cossack Regiments. 1827-1838

General. Don Host. 1829-1838

Field-grade Officer. Don Cossack Regiments. 1836-1844

Non-commissioned Officer and Cossack. Don Cossack Regiments. 1838-1845

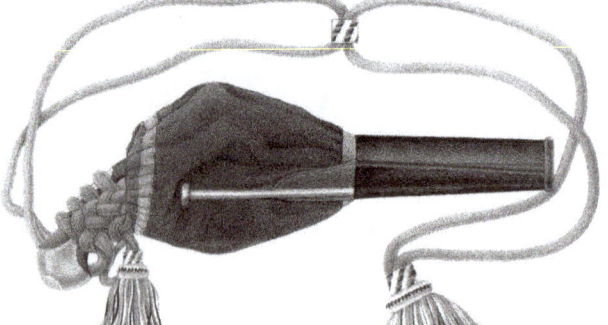

Lower Ranks' Bandolier for the Don Host, according to the pattern confirmed 29 April 1838

Lower Ranks' Pistol in Case for the Don Host, according to the pattern confirmed 29 April 1838

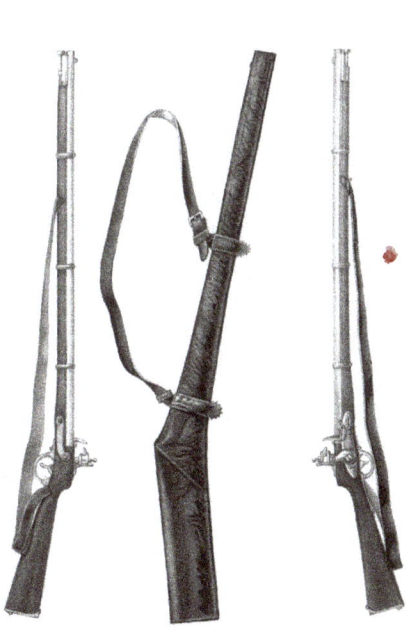

Lower Ranks' Shashka for the Don Host, according to the pattern confirmed 29 April 1838

Lower Ranks' Musket with Case for the Don Host, according to the pattern confirmed 29 April 1838

Field-grade Officer and Company-grade Officer. Don Cossack Regiments. 1838-1845

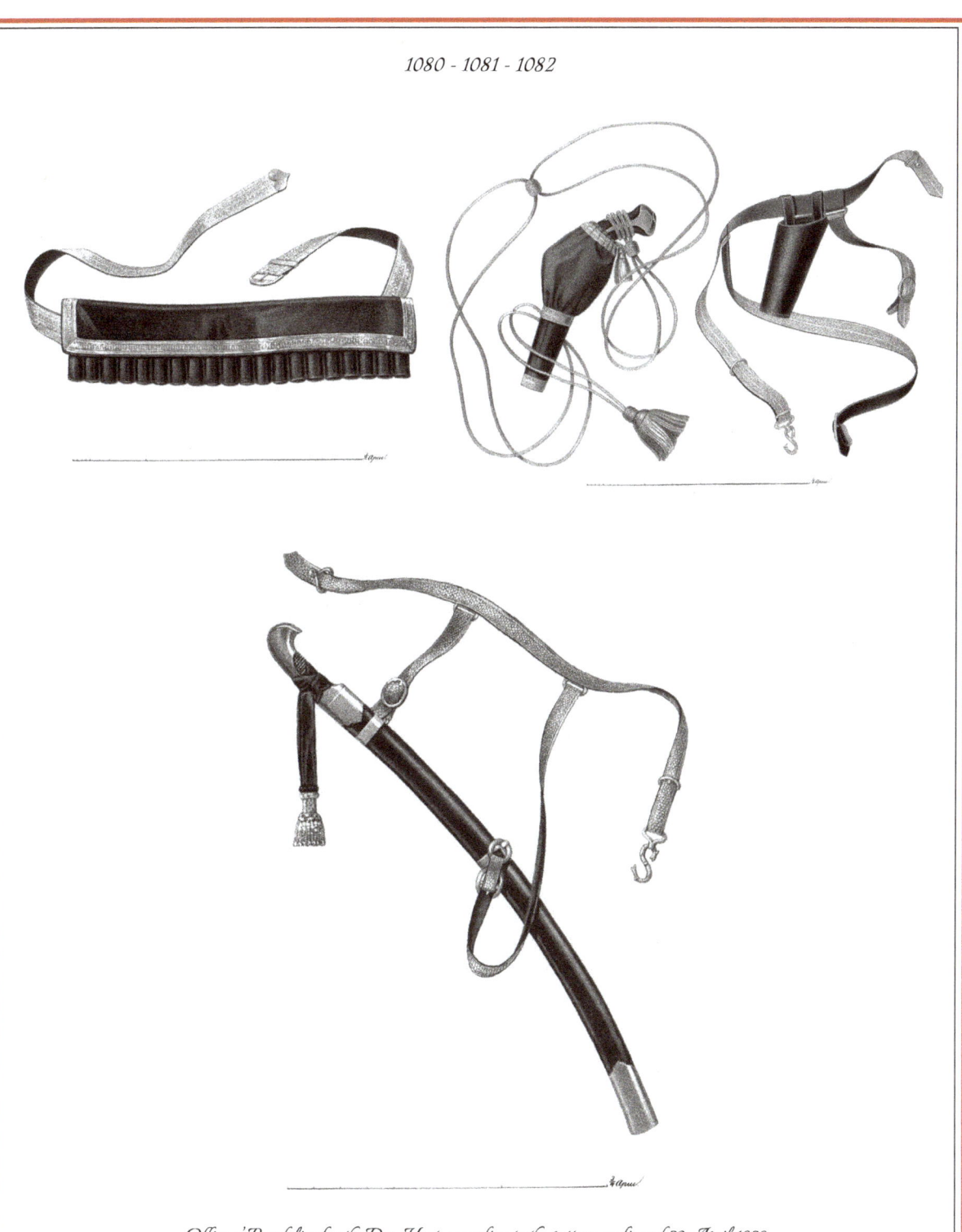

Officers' Bandolier for the Don Host, according to the pattern confirmed 29 April 1838
Officers' Pistol for the Don Host, according to the pattern confirmed 29 April 1838
Officers' Shashka for the Don Host, according to the pattern confirmed 29 April 1838

Cossack and Company-grade Officer. Don Cossack Regiments. 1838-1855

Foot and Horse Cossacks. Don Host on Internal Duty. 1838-1855

Orderlies. Don Host Youths at the Novocherkassk Hospital. 1841-1855

Field-grade Officer. Don Cossack Regiments. 1844

Cossack. Don Cossack Regiments serving in the Caucasus. 1845-1855

Company-grade Officer and Cossack. Don Cossack Regiments. 1845-1855

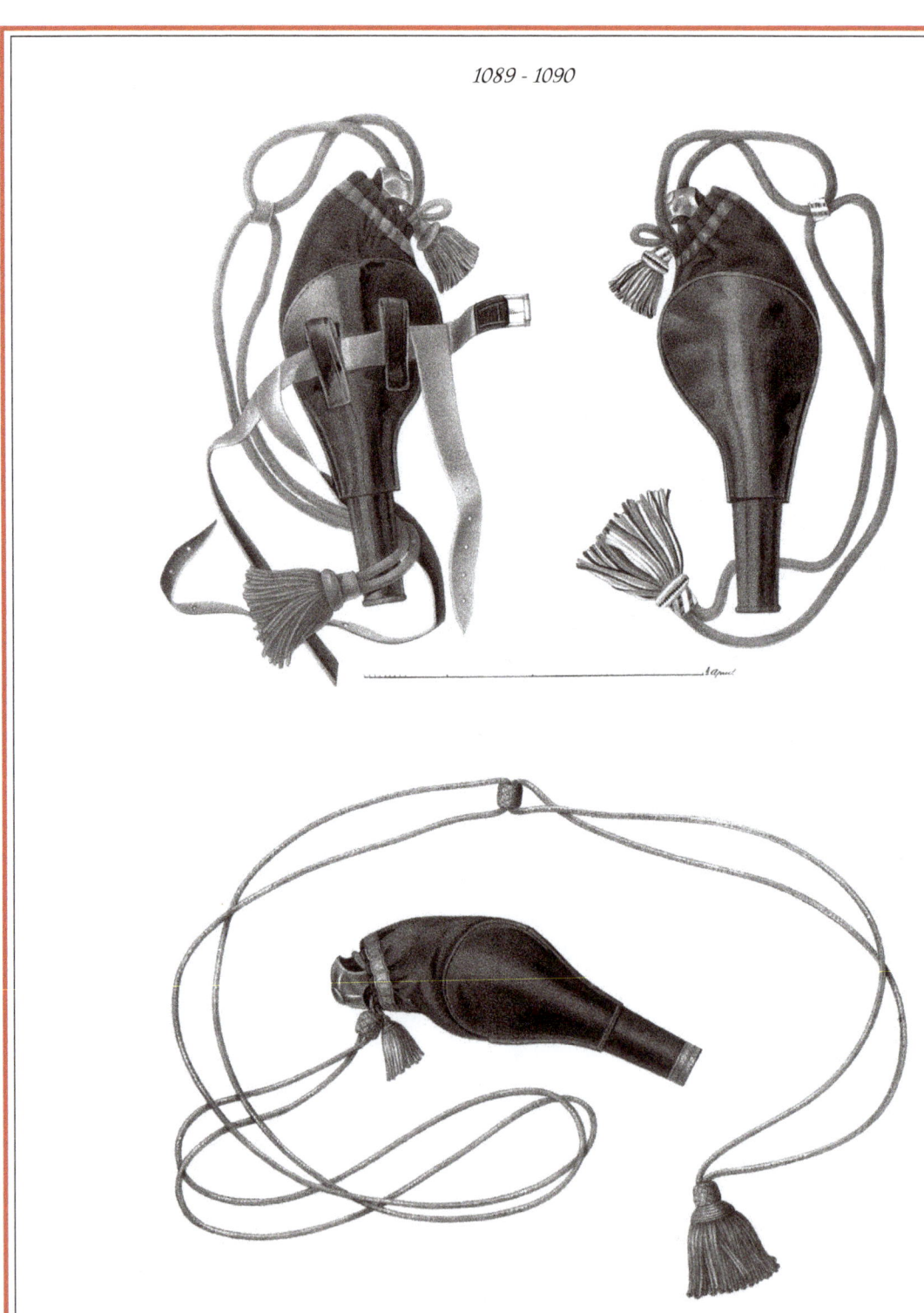

1089 - 1090

Lower Ranks' Pistol Case in the Don Host, according to the pattern confirmed 27 April 1845

Officers' Pistol Case for the Don Host, according to the pattern confirmed 27 April 1845

Lance Sling for Cossack Hosts, established 29 January 1849

Officers' Cossack Percussion Pistol, instituted 14 September 1849

Non-commissioned Officer. The Ataman HIS IMPERIAL HIGHNESS THE HEIR'S Regiment. 1827 and 1828

Company-grade Officer. The Ataman HIS IMPERIAL HIGHNESS THE HEIR'S Regiment. 1827 and 1828

Private. The Ataman HIS IMPERIAL HIGHNESS THE HEIR'S Regiment. 1828-1831

Company-grade Officers. The Ataman HIS IMPERIAL HIGHNESS THE HEIR'S Regiment. 1829-1831

Non-commissioned Officer. The Ataman HIS IMPERIAL HIGHNESS THE HEIR AND TSESAREVICH'S Regiment. 1831-1838

1098

Privates. The Ataman HIS IMPERIAL HIGHNESS THE HEIR AND TSESAREVICH'S Regiment. 1831-1838

Company-grade Officer. The Ataman HIS IMPERIAL HIGHNESS THE HEIR AND TSESAREVICH'S Regiment. 1831-1838

Company-grade Officer. The Ataman HIS IMPERIAL HIGHNESS THE HEIR AND TSESAREVICH'S Regiment. 1836-1844

Private. The Ataman HIS IMPERIAL HIGHNESS THE HEIR AND TSESAREVICH'S Regiment. 1838-1845

Parade Headdress Plate for Lower Ranks of the Ataman HIS IMPERIAL HIGHNESS THE HEIR AND
TSESAREVICH'S Regiment, established 29 April 1838
General-officers' Shabraque for the Don Host, established in 1837

Non-commissioned Officer. The Ataman HIS IMPERIAL HIGHNESS THE HEIR AND TSESAREVICH'S Regiment. 1838-1845

Field-grade Officer and Company-grade Officer. The Ataman HIS IMPERIAL HIGHNESS THE HEIR AND TSESAREVICH'S Regiment. 1838-1845

Company-grade Officer and Non-commissioned Officer. The Ataman HIS IMPERIAL HIGHNESS THE HEIR AND TSESAREVICH'S Regiment. 1844

Privates. The Ataman HIS IMPERIAL HIGHNESS THE HEIR AND TSESAREVICH'S Regiment. 1845-1855

Ammunition Pouch for Combatant Ranks of the Ataman HIS IMPERIAL HIGHNESS THE HEIR AND TSESAREVICH'S, established 27 April 1845

Officers' Cartridge-pouch for The Ataman HIS IMPERIAL HIGHNESS THE HEIR AND TSESAREVICH'S Regiment, established 18 January 1848

Trumpeter. The Ataman HIS IMPERIAL HIGHNESS THE HEIR AND TSESAREVICH'S Regiment. 1845-1855

Field-grade Officer. The Ataman HIS IMPERIAL HIGHNESS THE HEIR AND TSESAREVICH'S Regiment. 1845-1855

Private. The Ataman HIS IMPERIAL HIGHNESS THE HEIR AND TSESAREVICH'S Regiment. 1851-1855

Field-grade Officer. Life-Guards Cossack Regiment. 1829-1838

Private. Life-Guards Cossack Regiment. 1829-1838

Field-grade Officer. Life-Guards Cossack Regiment. (In vice-chekmen.) 1836-1844

Non-commissioned Officer and Private. Life-Guards Cossack Regiment. 1838-1845

Company-grade Officer. Life-Guards Cossack Regiment. 1838-1845

Non-commissioned Officer and Trumpeter. Life-Guards Cossack Regiment. 1845-1847

Private and Field-grade Officer. Life-Guards Cossack Regiment. 1845-1848

Non-commissioned Officer. Life-Guards Cossack Regiment. 1847-1855

Field-grade Officer. Life-Guards Cossack Regiment. 1848-1855

Cossack. Don Cossack Horse-Artillery Companies. 1827-1834

Company-grade Officer. Don Cossack Horse-Artillery Companies. 1827-1838

Cossack. Don Cossack Horse-Artillery Companies. 1829-1838

Company-grade Officer. Don Cossack Horse-Artillery Company No 3. 1830-1838

Cossack. Don Cossack Horse-Artillery Batteries. 1838-1845

Company-grade Officers. Don Cossack Horse-Artillery Batteries. 1838-1845

Cossack. Don Cossack Horse-Artillery Batteries. 1845-1855

Private. Life-Guards Don Horse-Artillery Company. 1830-1835

Company-grade Officer. Life-Guards Don Horse-Artillery Company. 1830-1834

Private. Life-Guards Don Horse-Artillery Battery. 1834

Company-grade Officer. Life-Guards Don Horse-Artillery Battery. 1834

Field-grade Officer. Life-Guards Don Horse-Artillery Battery. 1834-1838

Company-grade Officer. Life-Guards Don Horse-Artillery Battery. 1836-1844

Private. Life-Guards Don Horse-Artillery Battery. 1838-1845

Company-grade Officer. Life-Guards Don Horse-Artillery Battery. 1838-1845
Company-grade Officer. Life-Guards Don Horse-Artillery Battery. 1845-1855
Company-grade Officer. Life-Guards Don Horse-Artillery Battery. 1848-1855
Aide-de-Camp. Don Host. 1836-1845

Trumpeter. Life-Guards Don Horse-Artillery Battery. 1845-1855

General. Don Host. (In the standard general-officers' uniform.) 1837-1845

General-Adjutant and General of HIS IMPERIAL MAJESTY'S Suite. Don Host. 1837-1845

General-Adjutants' Parade Shabraque for the Don Host, established in 1837
Aides'-de-Camp Campaign Shabraque for the Don Host, established in 1837

1145

Field-grade Duty Officer. Don Host. 1837-1850

Adjutant, from the Life-Guards Cossack Regiment. 1837-1850

General-Adjutant. Don Host. 1844
Adjutant's Aide, from the Don Host. Host and Regional Duty Offices. 1844-1850
Field-grade Officer of the Don Host, serving in the Host's Internal Administration. 1846-1850
General of Guards Cossack units. 1849-1855

Field-grade Duty Officer. Don Host. 1850-1855

Cossack. Black Sea Cossack Host. 1827-1835

Company-grade Officer. Black Sea Cossack Host. 1827-1838

Cossack. Black Sea Cossack Host. 1835-1838

Non-commissioned Officer. Black Sea Cossack Host. 1838-1840

Field-grade Officer. Black Sea Cossack Host. 1838-1840

Cossack and Non-commissioned Officer. Horse Regiments of the Black Sea Cossack Host. 1840-1855

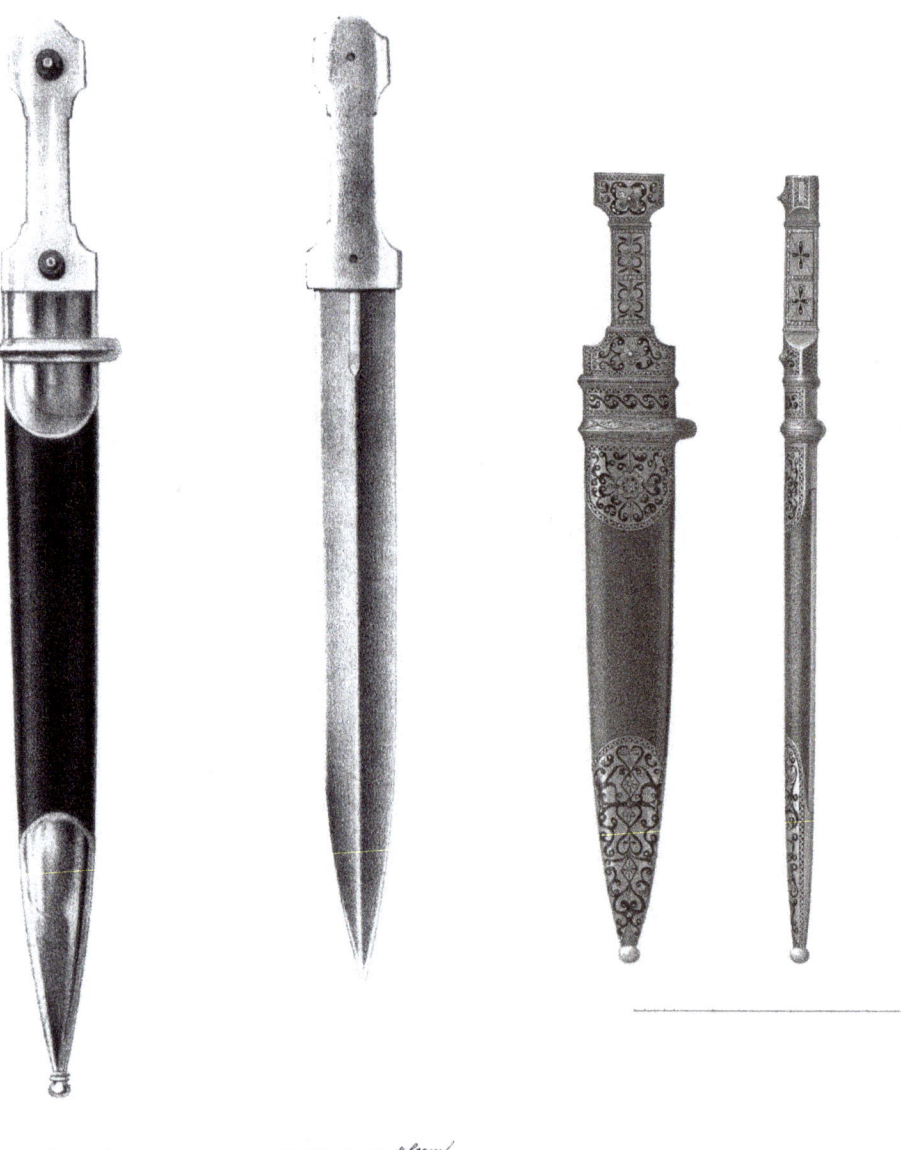

Kinzhal for Combatant Lower Ranks of the Black Sea Cossack Host, according to the pattern confirmed 1 November 1840 and 1 February 1841

Kinzhal for Officers of the Black Sea Cossack Host, according to the pattern confirmed 1 November 1840 and 1 February 1841

Swordbelt for Combatant Lower Ranks of the Black Sea Cossack Host, according to the pattern confirmed 1 November 1840 and 1 February 1841
Musket Case for Combatant Lower Ranks of the Black Sea Cossack Host, according to the pattern confirmed 1 November 1840 and 1 February 1841

Company-grade Officer. Horse Regiments of the Black Sea Cossack Host. 1840-1855

δ вершковъ.

Swordbelt and Belt for Officers of the Black Sea Cossack Host, according to the pattern confirmed 1 November 1840 and 1 February 1841

Cossack and Non-commissioned Officer. Foot Battalions of the Black Sea Cossack Host. 1848

Company-grade Officer. Foot Battalions of the Black Sea Cossack Host. 1840-1848

Cossack. Horse Regiments of the Black Sea Cossack Host. 1848-1855

Trumpeter. Horse Regiments of the Black Sea Cossack Host. 1842-1855

Company-grade Officers. Horse Regiments of the Black Sea Cossack Host. 1842-1844

Cossack and Drummer. Foot Battalions of the Black Sea Cossack Host. 1842-1848

Horse Cossack. Black Sea Cossack Host, on Internal Duty. 1844-1855

Cossack and Field-grade Officer. Foot Battalions of the Black Sea Cossack Host. 1848-1855

Cossack. Foot Battalions of the Black Sea Cossack Host. 1848-1855

Bugler. Foot Battalions of the Black Sea Cossack Host. 1854-1855

Private. Life-Guards Black Sea Cossack Squadron. 1829-1838

Private. Life-Guards Black Sea Cossack Squadron. 1838-1840

Company-grade Officer. Life-Guards Black Sea Cossack Squadron. 1838-1840

Private and Non-commissioned Officer. Life-Guards Black Sea Cossack Squadron. 1840-1845

Trumpeters. Life-Guards Black Sea Cossack Squadron. 1840-1845

Company-grade Officer. Life-Guards Black Sea Cossack Squadron. 1840-1845

Company-grade Officer. Life-Guards Black Sea Cossack Squadron. 1840-1842

Company-grade Officer. Life-Guards Black Sea Cossack Battalion. 1844-1855.
Non-commissioned Officer. Foot Garrison Artillery Company of the Black Sea Cossack Host. 1840-1845
Private. Life-Guards Black Sea Cossack Battalion. 1840-1845
Field-grade Officer. Life-Guards Black Sea Cossack Battalion. 1845-1855

Cossack. Horse-Artillery Company of the Black Sea Cossack Host. 1827-1838

Company-grade Officer. Horse-Artillery Company of the Black Sea Cossack Host. 1827-1838

Cossack. Horse-Artillery Battery of the Black Sea Cossack Host. 1838-1840

Cossack. Horse-Artillery Batteries of the Black Sea Cossack Host. 1840-1845

Trumpeter. Horse-Artillery Batteries of the Black Sea Cossack Host. 1840-1845

Company-grade Officer. Horse-Artillery Batteries of the Black Sea Cossack Host. 1840-1845
Non-commissioned Officer. Foot Garrison Artillery Company of the Black Sea Cossack Host. 1840-1845
Company-grade Officer. Horse-Artillery Batteries of the Black Sea Cossack Host. 1842-1845
Adjutant, from the Black Sea Cossack Host. 1851-1855

SOLDIERS, WEAPONS & UNIFORMS ALREADY PUBLISHED
(SOME TITLES)

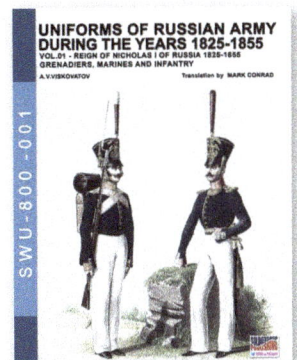
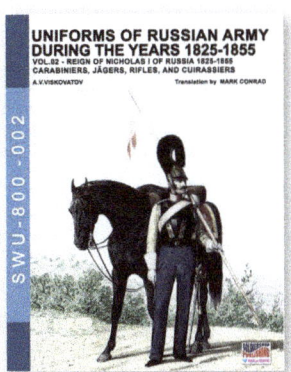
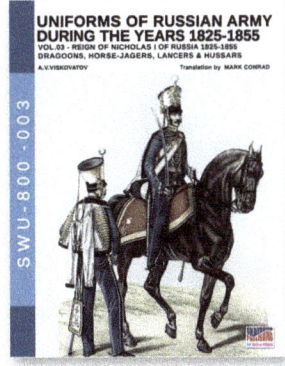
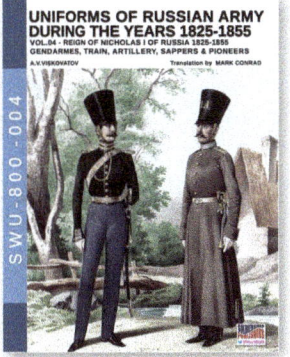

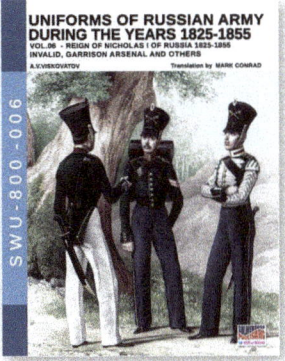

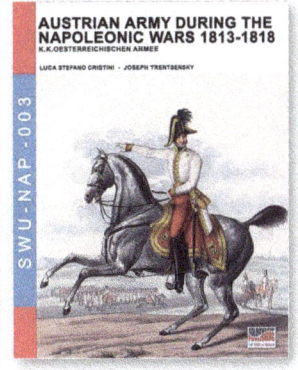
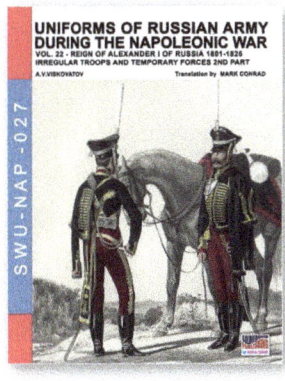

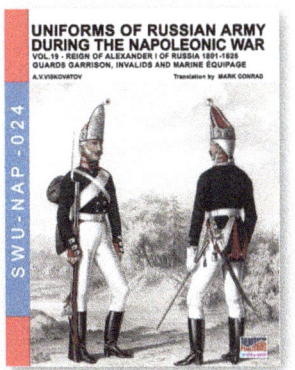